Rejoicing

Bruno Latour

———

REJOICING

Or the Torments of Religious Speech

Translated by Julie Rose

polity

Donald Wesling
2013–2014

First published in French as *Jubiler* © Les Empêcheurs de penser en rond/
Le Seuil, 2002
This translation copyright © Polity Press, 2013

Polity Press
65 Bridge Street
Cambridge CB2 1UR, UK

Polity Press
350 Main Street
Malden, MA 02148, USA

**INSTITUT
FRANÇAIS**

This book is supported by the Institut français
as part of the Burgess programme.
(www.frenchbooksnews.com).

ISBN-13: 978-0-7456-6006-6
ISBN-13: 978-0-7456-6007-3 (pb)

A catalogue record for this book is available from the British Library.

Typeset in 11 on 14 pt Sabon
by Servis Filmsetting Ltd, Stockport, Cheshire
Printed and bound in Great Britain by the MPG Printgroup

The publisher has used its best endeavours to ensure that the URLs for
external websites referred to in this book are correct and active at the time
of going to press. However, the publisher has no responsibility for the
websites and can make no guarantee that a site will remain live or that the
content is or will remain appropriate.

Every effort has been made to trace all copyright holders, but if any have
been inadvertently overlooked the publisher will be pleased to include any
necessary credits in any subsequent reprint or edition.

For further information on Polity, visit our website: www.politybooks.com

Rejoicing – or the torments of religious speech: that is what he wants to talk about, that is what he can't actually seem to talk about: it's as though the cat had got his tongue; as though he was spoilt for choice when it comes to words; as though it was impossible to articulate; he can't actually seem to share what, for so long, he has held so dear to his heart; before his nearest and dearest, he is forced to cover up; he can only stutter; how can he own up to his friends, to his colleagues, his nephews, his students?

He is ashamed of not daring to speak out and ashamed of wanting to speak out, regardless. Ashamed, too, for those who don't make it any easier for him, thrusting his head underwater while claiming to rescue him, or, instead of throwing him a lifebuoy, throwing words as heavy as a mooring buoy at him. Weighted with lead, that's it – they've weighted him with lead. Yes, he goes to mass, and often, on Sunday, but it doesn't mean anything. Alas, no, it doesn't *mean* anything really; it *can't* mean anything anymore to anyone. There is no way of saying these things anymore, no tone, no tonality, no regime of speech or utterance. It's a twisted situation: he is ashamed of what he hears on Sunday from the pulpit when he goes to mass; but ashamed, too, of the incredulous hatred or amused indifference of those who laugh at anyone who goes to church. Ashamed that he goes, ashamed of not daring to say he goes. He grinds

1

his teeth when he hears the things said inside; but he boils with rage when he hears the things said outside. All that's left for him to do is hang his head, weary, sheepish, before the horrors and misconceptions on the inside as well as before the horrors and misconceptions on the outside; it's a double cowardice, double shame, and he has no words to express this, as though he were caught between two opposing currents, with the resultant clash leaving him whirling on the spot.

It is not of the religious that he wants to speak, not of the fact of religion. It is not of that vast stratum of institutions, law, psychology, rituals, politics, art, cultures, monuments and myths; of what for so long and in all climates took hold of human beings obliged to band together in conglomerations and attend to the things connecting them – *link* and *scruple* being the two etymological senses of the word *religio*. The only thing he wants to reactivate is religious utterance, that very strange habit which developed over the course of history in the form of the Word, and which seems to him today to be so horribly confused. He doesn't want to study either the religious or religion – still less, *religions* plural – but only to disinter a form of expression that used to be so free and inventive, fruitful and saving in days gone by, but that now dries on his tongue whenever he tries to recover its movement, excitement, its structure. Why does what used to be so alive for him turn deadly boring whenever he endeavours to talk about it to others – his children, for instance? What monstrous metamorphosis makes what once had so much meaning become absolutely *meaningless*, like a blast of words freezing on the lips of convicts in the Siberian cold?

2

What he would need to do, first and foremost, is be able to escape the menacing choice that vulgar common sense demands of anyone who sets out to talk about religion: 'But are you a believer or a non-believer?' He'd like to able to answer: 'Obviously, I'm speaking as a non-believer.' But what he'd mean by that word 'non-believer' is someone who no longer believes in belief in any way, a true *agnostic*. Well, this belief in belief is something that those inside share with those outside – it's actually how they manage to distinguish the inside from the outside. If there's one thing both sides agree on, it is that this line can be drawn to mark their difference: 'You believe in it, I don't believe in it.' How, then, can we say that it has absolutely nothing to do with belief? And especially not with believing *in* something, in someone, in the unnameable, the unprofferable G. How can we make it clear that belief or non-belief in G. makes no difference when it comes to talking about these things, to talking *starting with* these things? That that is not where the problem lies, that it actually entails mixing up categories, misdirecting ideas, committing an error of syntax, a blurring of genres? Yes, in these matters of religion (for brevity's sake, we can keep the word), belief in G. is absolutely not involved and, so, cannot define any kind of boundary between believers and non-believers, the faithful and the infidels. This fact already somewhat clouds the message he wants to get out before he's even begun. So it's hardly surprising he has some trouble speaking, since to hear him you have to be an agnostic: neither indifferent nor sceptical, but quite determined, when it comes to talking about religion again, to do without the poison of belief. Who's up for such asceticism?

Especially when he'd like to make such a statement without shocking? And without shocking *twice*: first the faithful, then the infidels; first the believers, then the non-believers, those on the inside and those on the outside. He's well aware that anyone seeking to scandalize would be better off tying a millstone round his neck and throwing himself into a pond. If it was just a matter of choosing sides, it would be easy, everyone would line up in battle formation and he would bravely fire a shot as well as the next man. He would either return to the bosom of his holy mother the Church, bravely lambasting the non-believers and battling against indifference and heresy; or he would join the vast army of critics, railing against the sins of irrationality, against the 'resurgence of fundamentalisms' (at the rear, safely away from the front line, as an arbiter, journalist or savant, he could also keep score). But that's just it: for him, there is no front. Neither belief nor non-belief distinguishes those who talk about religion from those who don't. That is why he doesn't want to scandalize either those who hold on to belief in belief in 'God' as their most precious good, or those who preserve belief in non-belief in 'God' as their most sacred right. An impossible task, of course, since they are at loggerheads: what satisfies one camp will necessarily shock the other.

With such demands, how can he possibly write clear and straight? He'd like to talk about religion again, not to believe in belief, but not to scandalize, either. Such an iron collar weighs so heavily on his shoulders that he loses his footing and thrashes about in the muddy waters. Every time he opens his mouth to speak, he swallows water, then spits out toads and sticky seaweed.

4

If he hopes to avoid wounding, he'll have to tread so lightly that he leaves no trace in the sand; his handling will have to be so deft no one will feel the scalpel going in; he'll have to choose his words so carefully that, no matter how strange they are, they always sound right. As for the keyboard of his computer, an angel will have to come and tap away at it. What can earthlings like him do? And yet, he finally takes the plunge. Too late now to back-paddle: it's sink or swim.

And this is where he must raise a second difficulty, and do so without causing pain, the way a clever nurse rips off a painful bandage in a single swift gesture: not only does the gesture of faith make no difference, but neither does its object, 'God'. In ancient times, when people talked about the gods, believers were no more numerous than non-believers. The presence of divinities was obvious in the air or the soil. They formed the common fabric of people's lives, the primary material of all rituals, the indisputable reference point of all existence, the ordinary fodder of all conversation. Well, it's not like that anymore – at least, not in the wealthy countries of the West. The common fabric of our lives, our primary material, our ordinary fare, our indisputable framework, if there is such a thing, is the *non-existence* of gods sensitive to prayer and ruling over our destinies. Quick, rip off the bandage before the pain can be felt: that's all to the good! You don't talk any better about religion starting from the existence of G. than starting from the non-existence of G. It makes no difference, since that's not what it's about – at least, not in that way, not within that tonal range, not in that spirit.

If we really wanted to translate into today's

vocabulary what people once used to talk about when they uttered the word 'God', we'd have to look not to some new being we could substitute for him, but rather to whatever it is that gives everyone the same feeling of indisputable familiarity. For most of our contemporaries, expressions such as 'the non-existence of God', 'the banality of the world', 'indifferent matter', 'market consumerism', would be good synonyms since what would be referred to thereby would be the same obviousness, the same everyday reality, the same easiness, the same solid backing. Religious talk latches onto either term, 'God' or 'non-God', without distinction, since it needs to begin with an accepted reference point which it will shake and then rattle, in a bid to get it to say something completely different. So, the meaning of the word G. does not derive from the name chosen as point of departure but from the shake-up that ensues. It doesn't matter whether this discourse begins, in ancient times, with the familiar face of a helpful 'God' to whom you could talk through rituals, or, as today, with a 'non-God' deaf to rituals whom it would be quite mad to address prayers to: the only thing that counts is what it will cause you to be subjected to as a result of the evidence of common sense, the alarming twisting that ordinary certainties will undergo. To confuse belief (or non-belief) in 'God' with the demands of religion means taking the decor for the room, the overture for the opera. It doesn't matter what is in the beginning: the only thing that counts is what comes just after.

There you are, he's got himself into a proper tangle. Before he's really even got started, he's probably already shocked those on the inside as much as those on the outside. 'What!' they cry as one. 'In religion, God is not the issue?!' No, actually, but he's going to have to think and start all over again. It's impossible to simplify. There is no straight path. No angelic inspiration, no muse whispering in your ear. No well of clear water springing up beneath your feet. Once you attempt to start talking about these things again, you need to develop capacities for *discernment* that can only be acquired through various mortifications, the stubborn repetition of rituals, relentless pursuit of appropriate concepts. In these matters, you can't rely on intuition. And there's an added, contradictory, demand, which is that you not get bogged down in pointless complications: a child of seven should be able to understand everything. Every word must have a beguiling, a biblical, simplicity (even if the person who came up with the second adjective most certainly hadn't read the Scriptures . . .). You can see why so many people turn away from this ungodly language game and abandon it, shrugging their shoulders. Better to keep quiet or to trot out the same old things, or send yourself up. There's no means now of saying what is at issue. Or, rather, the means of talking both simply and subtly about religious matters have been taken from us. Those means have become either complicated, archaeological, scholarly, or so inane, religiose, simplistic, that you can only cry in pity over them. How can we go back over this fork in the road, retrace the route that leads to this crossroads?

Maybe the requirement of not scandalizing anyone in the slightest is too heavy, and we need to lift it to be able to speak a bit freely. The fact is there are true and false scandals, true and false translations, and we really need

7

to learn how to distinguish between them, otherwise no utterance will be audible. Differentiating, contrasting, verifying, accepting, rejecting – there is no other way. There is no truthfulness without meticulous sorting. There are indeed artificial scandals that we really need to point out, even if it means shocking those who take them for the very kernel of their faith. In religion as in science, there are *artefacts* that must be carefully dismantled. It's just that time passes, words that once had a meaning lose it. But, you see, the people whose job it is to change words so as to keep the meaning, clerics, have preferred piously to preserve the words at the risk of losing the meaning; they've left us, the rest of us, we latecomers, ignoramuses, stutterers, equipped with words that have become untruthful for the purposes of recording the real things we hold dear to our hearts.

For instance, the word 'God', which once served as the premise of all arguing, could have been translated, when ways of life changed, as 'indisputable framework of ordinary existence' so that we could continue to really see that what was thereby designated was merely the preliminary and prelude to a conversion of meaning. But instead of this direct, painless, progressive translation, they started clinging for dear life to the term 'God' and pitting it against 'non-God', without seeing that they were dealing with two forms about as different as *God*, *Deus* and *Theos* for translating the same everyday reality. Thinking they were protecting their heritage, they squandered it. Thinking they were doing the right thing and protecting 'God' against 'the rise of atheism', they didn't see that, as this slow drift of tectonic plates progressed, they were little by little substituting one word for another. The term was kept for too long and turned into a nasty scandal; it was now giving off a pestilential smell. Once an indifferent preliminary, it had become a major obstacle to understanding. Whereas in the past no one baulked at the word 'God' when it was shared as the starting point of all discourse, they turned it into a stumbling block that allowed them to judge the loyalty of the faithful. They made a scandal of something that used not to cause anyone to stumble. Alas, they carried their perversity a lot further than that: they thought that this scandal, artificially produced, was positive, that they'd be rewarded according to the force with which they preserved the old term 'against the dirty tricks, the downward spirals, the compromises of the age', that they would be assured of dying in the odour of sanctity, that this was what they would be judged by at Judgement Day. They believed themselves to be faithful when they were in fact abandoning the meaning (as a familiar preliminary to whatever keeps us all gathered together), which slowly, surreptitiously, gradually, went from the old term 'God' to its new formulation 'non-God'. What they should have done was the opposite, they should have leapt with all their worldly goods into the new language game before it was too late; by keeping the word, they lost the treasure that the new term was to protect. Whosoever will save his life shall lose it [Matthew 16:25].

To revive the language, to learn again clumsily how to speak right, we'd have to be able to say: atheism forms just as perfect a point of departure as belief 'in God'. And even a preferable point of departure – since it provides an indisputable framework for common

9

action and thereby more closely resembles the expression 'helpful God', from the days when people raised their hands towards the heavens in the presence of misfortune – than any current invocation to a 'God' whose life-form has passed. But how can we utter this phrase without scandalizing either those for whom 'God' is an obvious fact or those for whom 'non-God' is an obvious fact – the first, because they believe that only the beginning matters, the second, because they don't want to hear what follows? He is committed to not shocking on both fronts; so he has to avoid impious new inventions as much as ghastly apologetics, all the while distinguishing with the utmost care between shocks necessary to understanding the message and artificial scandals that get in the way of understanding that message. By dint of piling on all these contradictory demands, he is going to make himself dumb; by dint of wearing his eyes out trying to distinguish between true and false scandals, he is going to make himself myopic. Yet, he has no other option than to keep going. Meaning is lost if you stop gathering it, collecting it – *religiere*, as the Latin says, speaking of religion. But to do this, you always have to start again from scratch, say the same things in a completely different idiom – yes, the same things; yes, but in a completely different idiom. The first time you hear it, any fresh revival of an old theme will necessarily sound shrill, intolerable, inaudible, cacophonous. You have first to get the ear used to the new sound, to the revival in a new key of the exact same old tune.

'There is no God', says the sensible man in his heart of hearts, and that's all to the good: everything is cleaner, more precise, more definite. And so, there is no belief *in* G. anymore either. That is the sticking point; his tongue forks once more, it's forked like the devil's feet, within spitting distance of his perdition, and yet he has to go down that perilous path, he has to go through that narrow gateway: we can no longer address ourselves in the *vocative* case to someone who might hear us, listen to us and console us. We are no longer like children, talking loudly in the dark to stop from being frightened. The 'God' we once invoked no longer has hands, or eyes, or ears, and his mouth is forever sealed.

In the little church of Montcombroux, built in the year 1000, when I speak, on my own, it's my voice I hear, my voice alone, and words fail me, alas, for none of the prayers presented to the pilgrim on little cards eaten into by the damp corresponds anymore to the language game in which I wish to find myself involved. It would be so easy, of course, to fall sobbing before some pillar and, faltering, trust to the invocation: 'Thou, O "my God", hear my prayer' – but what a lie that would be, what a piece of fraud, for I would then lose those who haven't followed me into the nave, those who'd laugh at me, those who believe I believe, that I invoke and pray. And I have to go on addressing them, equally. The temptation has to be resisted. I've got better things to do than return to the fold, for it's no longer one sheep that's gone astray, the whole flock has been lost along the way, together with the mountain pasture, the valley, the mountain range, the entire continent; yes, it's up to the shepherd to rejoin the flock, it's up to the fold, the sheepfold, the farm, the village, to set off once again and make up for lost time, to regain the Promised Land they left behind, lying fallow. Is it my fault if I'm forced to address a 'non-God' through prayer, as they did in the days when the presence of a consoling 'God' was taken for granted? If I'm required to recite the same words in the silence of a country church as those words which, a thousand years earlier, stirred the Bourbonnais peasants who had come to protect their harvests during Rogation time? The world has 'lost faith', as they say? No, 'Faith' has lost the world.

The second person singular 'thou' used to have the force of an obvious fact, but those days are over. The invocation dries on my tongue. I can't say it. It sticks in my throat. So what's to be done now? Should I go away? Admire the Roman vault? Bemoan the restoration work? Aestheticize? Historicize? Touristicize? Mythologize? Demythologize? No, wait a bit, let's try again, sit back down. I manage to murmur, shaking with fear and ridiculousness: 'I address thee, thou who don't exist. I address myself alone, I who don't exactly exist either, and I know full well that I'm no longer master and owner of my words, that thou has no presence beyond my broken voice stammering under the vault.'

Could we hear ourselves at this price? Hear ourselves speak? Double abandonment: of the vocative which has become impossible ever since 'non-God' took up residence on earth; of mastery of language by a free subject in full control of himself. Of course it's I and I alone who am speaking: do you take me for a madman who thinks he's addressing some absent being who might answer him through the intermediary of silent stones? Of course it's I who am speaking when I speak: do you take me for a madman who lives in the illusion of self-transparency

12

and who might know in advance what is going to come out of his mouth? Not in front of, not above, not inside, but beside, askew, coiled in my hesitant speech act, another hesitation is raving. No, it's not the returned echo of my words, for an echo would repeat, simply amplified or distorted, what I've cried out; no, it's not ventriloquism, for the conjuror controls both voices, his and the one he so cleverly projects towards another body; no, it's not bad faith getting me to mistake for a foreign voice what another part of me is softly uttering. No one is speaking but me, but all the same, this me has become all twisted, it's not itself, it's surprised, slightly alienated, let's say, rather, *altered*. What has happened? Weird things are being said in here. How am I going to express my surprise in the face of these words that I utter without knowing I'm going to say them?

Sympathize with me now in my misery: to articulate the first language game, the one involving the consoling 'God', the faithful have at their disposal six thousand years of poets, preachers, inspired psalmists; to articulate the second, the game involving non-control of words, I have nothing, no breviary, no psalter, no song book, not the smallest image, nothing but myself, I who am nothing – not even a believer. And yet, the old term has indeed become unutterable, unsituatable, unjustifiable – except inside the narrow fold, among those in the habit of praying among themselves. Now, what I really need is something new, I need that psalter no one has set to verse, that collection of songs no one has compiled, of holy pictures no one has coloured in. It's not surprising that I'm dying of thirst, that my tongue is coated with dust and sticks to the roof of my mouth. All the words offered to me to introduce me to prayer assume prior acquiescence to a language that has become foreign. It's not the object of prayer that has died out, it's the prayer form itself that has become outmoded. And if I did finally decide to read the naive lines written under the awful plaster statues, I would become an impostor twice over: if I uttered them, when they no longer have any meaning; if I didn't utter them, when I find myself alone in a church, in summer, praying prayerlessly, before these icons. Whether I speak or keep silent, I'm forced into blasphemy: I say G.'s name in vain.

You who are on the inside, don't condemn my lack of faith too quickly; you who are on the outside, don't be too quick to mock my overcredulity; you who are indifferent, don't be too quick to wax ironic about my perpetual hesitations. Think of all the *arrears* I have to pay on top of the words, formulae, turns of phrase that I draw out of my meagre fund: yes, arrears, deficits, unpaid translation debts. Changes of epochs have caused the strata of discourse to slide, slowly and inexorably, just like the rocky plates along the San Andreas fault line, so much so that half the church now finds itself several dozen metres away from the other half. All that's left is two gaping ruins: the one for sheltering the people on the inside, the other only good for expelling the people on the outside. How many centuries ago did you stop rebuilding the nave to prevent it collapsing? Stop shifting it out of line and propping it up again without let-up, the never-ending resumption of work accompanying the slow shearing away that more and more contorts the gaping lips of the fault? Two, three, four, ten centuries? Even if you've only left it ten years, two years, two days, that would be enough for the edifice to break up. But several centuries? Can you measure the extent of the deficit? Can you imagine the mountain of debts that this represents? How do you expect me to reimburse these late fees all on my own, to pay back this vertiginous hole that's been found in the accounts? The church no longer holds together, the words no longer have meaning.

In ceasing to translate we have ceased to preserve, and this is what has thrown the word mill, the prayer mill, out of gear. This is what we need to return to, this particular mishap, to see if we can't repair the machine, the machine for grinding out religion. It's the only way I can pay my debts and start reimbursing the huge deficit I've lumbered myself with. You say it's not mine? I'm not responsible for it? Oh yes, I am! For here I am, trying once more, after hesitating for ages, to loosen up the phrases in my mouth, to shake up that herd of cattle, and not just a single bullock, that's sitting on my tongue, causing me to keep my own counsel. Anyway, it's my heritage, I've come to claim it, and too bad if I find it mortgaged to the hilt. Once the debts have been discharged, the treasure I've been bequeathed will, I'm sure, redeem them a hundredfold. I can already see the gold shining in the gestures handed down, I can hear the clinking of the wonders amassed in the treasure chest, even if it is carried from mass to mass without being any better understood by its commentators than security guards profit from the billions they risk their lives lugging around. In the days of anti-Semitic Church teachings, medieval sculptors represented the Synagogue blindfolded, handing down to the Christians the Book it

15

could no longer understand despite having written it. With what thick masks, what veils, what catafalques would we have to represent the Churches handing down the treasure of the Scriptures today without trying to interpret them anymore?

And yet the Scriptures have been properly and faithfully handed down. Anyone can hear them. But then the sermon begins – and the overburdened listener feels like running away as fast as his legs will carry him, for what he fears finding is that, in accepting this heritage, he's made a bad deal. He tells himself he should have declared himself incompetent like so many people he now begins to admire for their good sense, shrewdness, honesty – or business acumen, at least. How right they were to leave religion to its own devices! If you have to stomach such interpretations, such religiosity, fill up the attic with so much old junk, you'd be better off letting the precious repository be sold to the highest bidder at a public auction. And yet, a second later, I'm caught again. The gold shines again beneath the inanities. I regain confidence, determined to understand the mystery of this apparatus, as rickety, unstable and changeable as it is. No, definitely not, no mountain of debt will make me give up my heritage. I covet the treasure hidden from those on the inside as much as from those on the outside, from the vendors who no longer know the value of what they are offering as much as from the buyers who laugh at this old flea-market stuff.

The machine's mechanism can't be that complicated: 'Avoid paraphrasing and straying off-subject' – any schoolchild, writing his first commentary, learns that from his master's mouth. You either rehash it or repeat it; you either say the same thing a second time or you say the same thing differently – unless you lose yourself in thorny reflections instead. There is no interpretation without renewal. No word is taken up again as is, but the meaning, on the other hand, does circulate again. So, translating 'helpful God' in an idiom we can understand today, we need to say 'obvious framework of ordinary everyday existence'; repeating the term 'God' would amount to paraphrasing and rehashing, since we'd have lost the sense of what was once meant: the guaranteed reference point of our common existence. In believing ourselves faithful, we would have betrayed the meaning. We would have broken the second commandment: 'Thou shalt not take the Lord G.'s name in vain.' Who could fight that terrible injunction? How could we not tremble before the falseness, the vanity of our invocations, if we lose ourselves in the translation, in the repetition, the reiteration of the holy name? If our tongue has been forked and we've mistaken the rehashed word for the repeated word, the paraphrased word for the word commented on, the (apparently) faithful word for the (truly) faithful word, the (truly) unfaithful word for the (apparently) unfaithful word?

'That's all very well,' the student charged with writing his commentary frostily replies, 'but how am I supposed to distinguish the vain paraphrase from the fruitful interpretation?' Silence on the part of the teacher. There is no rule. No trick. You have to run the same risk every time and it will be different every time. The difference between rehashing and repeating is so fine that only an angel could slip through the gap, but the devil, too, can worm his way into those infinitesimal nuances: *lapsus*

17

calami, a slip of the pen. What if I'm guilty of serious betrayal? I claim to follow closely the meaning I've reaped and recast in other formulae, other terms that are not only different but contrary to the ones we started with; I invoke the difference between the letter that killeth and the spirit that giveth life [II Corinthians 3:6]. But if I abandon word-for-word repetition of the same terms, if I let go of the solid support of the handrail, how can I be sure that the *transformation* I've performed has kept the meaning *intact*? What if I've lost the meaning along the way, dropped the substance for the shadow, mislaid the spirit every bit as much as the letter? That would mean I'd lost discernment. And that's when I'd have invoked G.'s name in vain. If I've truly scandalized, then I'm not worth the rope that will hang me.

I can't get out of it by behaving as though there were solid rules for translating, or, conversely, as though what was involved here was an unfathomable mystery forever beyond words that ought to have been entrusted to superior authorities: I have to succeed in understanding what a *transformation through a translation that maintains the meaning intact* means. The machine can only be fixed at this price. It's not obscure, but it is a bit on the subtle side. Or rather, such infantile subtlety has become obscure to us because of the translation arrears that those in charge of us, our tutors, forgot to acquit when they handed down our assets mortgaged to the hilt. Can we raise those mortgages?

Words fail him once again, but this time it's because he has to talk here about *science*, not religion, and that form of words, however modern, however prestigious, is even more misunderstood, even more obscure than the other form. In fact, it's from the sciences, for the last four centuries at least, that we've taken the model for transformations that maintain relationships intact. Move around a cube drawn inside the space of descriptive geometry and no matter how you turn it, skew it, project it, none of its relationships will be lost, even if appearances are drastically altered every time. Computer-assisted design, movie special effects, taxi GPS screens offering computerized map-reading have familiarized us all with such transformation spaces. The form is always different, but something – constants – survives all such distortions. From the creation of humble perspective in the paintings of the Renaissance to the sublime transformations of general relativity, it is always a question of abandoning perishable matter in order to preserve intact a formal constant which alone is judged to be essential, most often calculable. Only at this price do we obtain *in-formation* about something – that is, most precisely, what survives *in* the *form* while we gradually throw out what, in contrast, turns into matter.

A map doesn't look like the actual territory mapped, but it preserves several relationships – angles, proportions, place names, writing conventions – which, once we're back on the ground, allow us, through a reverse translation process, to find ourselves in familiar territory. The sign 'Montcombroux-le-Vieux, 1.5 km' doesn't look anything like the general staff map or the winding path that leads to the town, yet the three forms of matter, sliding together, fitting together, one into the other, preserve relationships of distance that you can check as you sweat away on your bicycle thanks to various documents and signs. Flitting from one trace to another, your eye allows you to draw a reference path. The term '1.5 km' *refers* so clearly to something beyond itself that it allows you to attain that thing in thought, thereby offering in advance access to a pathway unknown to the cyclist. This term possesses truth value. Thanks to this kind of series of documents, it becomes possible to know, to master; we dominate by sight, we embrace by eye; we begin to articulate verifiable utterances about the world since we can say whether a sentence is true or false.

Is this how religious translation works? Is this how the student should work his commentary? No, of course not, and this is where things get horribly complicated, or, more exactly, monstrously *distorted*, as in anamorphosis. We might as well admit it straight away: there is no information in matters of religion, no maintenance of constants, no transfers of relationships intact throughout the stream of transformations. And so, sadly, no knowledge of the kind the humblest map provides, no science, no reference, no access, no mastery, no control, nothing we can dominate by sight. There's no point trying to get around this rule: the connection between a religious text and the thing it talks about is not the same as the connection between a map and its territory. Not even the connection between a secret, encrypted, scrambled, deliberately concealed map and a distant world only vaguely glimpsed. It's very simple: those texts, those words do not provide *access* to anything whatever; they do not form the first link in a chain of reference that would, in the end, if all the links hold firm, allow us to find ourselves on familiar turf, to

have seen in advance what we were dealing with. No
control over the world thanks to some document that
would preserve the world's relationships. No hold. No
treasure hunts. No reversible path, either. Whereas we
travel along the pathways of information, going up and
down endlessly from map to territory and from territory
to map, covering the space in between with signs, posts
and landmarks the better to lessen the distance between
the successive layers of matter and thereby ensure maintenance of aspect ratios thanks to tighter and tighter
meshing, we can't go back over a religious translation,
retrace the way back so as to lessen the shock, reduce
the gulf, diminish the discrepancy. Impossible to turn a
blind eye: information doesn't use the same vehicles, the
same conduits, the same meandering courses as those
words that change, alter, shake up. There is no truth
value that can be calculated by a 'yes' or a 'no' – at least
not that kind of calculation, not that kind of value, not
that kind of truth, not that kind of yes or no.

But why was there any conflict between the meandering courses of scientific reference and the paths of
religious translation in the first place? Between the
search for constants via production of viable information and the search for versions capable of recreating
the original message? Those paths should never have
crossed. You can't begin to speak again without putting
an end to this comedy of errors that has made science
the very close enemy of religion. These two forms of
utterance depend on hard work that produces very fragile results, leaves traces so small, occupies space-time
so differently, creates such incommensurable ecological
niches that they had no more reason to begin to do

battle with each other than do moles with frogs. That this happened regardless meant not counting on a third thief who, in his clumsiness, got the reciprocal tasks of science and religion equally wrong, forcing them to enter into burlesque wars. We might call this particular madwoman in the attic *double-click communication*, in honour of the computer mouse.

The sciences, plural, the true sciences, the ones that allow us to study their laboratory life, teams and equipment, practise a risky form of meandering: everything they produce is paid for with a painful transformation, since the utterance never looks like the thing it refers to. But, for double-click communication, all difficulties vanish, all paths level out: information becomes faithful communication without any transformation whatsoever, through simple obvious likeness between the copy and the original. This is sheer fantasy, naturally: no science would be possible through imitation, transparency and faithfulness. And yet, because of a history that has no place here, the type of communication that comes under the heading 'Science', *singular*, has taken the place of the sciences, *plural*, thereby concealing their prodigious transformations. Double-click communication, this immediate and costless access, this conveyance that appears to demand no transformation, has itself become, for our contemporaries, the model of all possible communication, the ideal, the metric standard of all movement, the judge of all faithfulness, the guarantee of all truth. It is through association with such fabled transparency that we evaluate all other conveyances. Starting, of course, with religious speech, which becomes pitiful in comparison with this ideal, since it

22

can't convey anything without transforming it from top to bottom. But make no mistake: by this account the sciences themselves, those formidable products we're so proud of, would, if we had to judge them, too, by the yardstick of double-click communication, become exactly as dishonest, unfaithful, opaque, manipulative, deformed and artificial as religious utterance. They were simply lucky enough, due to political reasons having to do with the very organization of the modern world, for no one ever to have got around to describing them – until very recently.

To talk about religion again, others, worthier than he, received inspiration from on high, secret wounds marked their flanks, or some kind of holy unction oiled their foreheads. But no one appointed him, nothing marked him out, if not the certainty that once we modify, as he has done (as he thinks he has done), the common version of the sciences, everything else can start to change – first and foremost, religion. The thing that allows him to speak, the thing that gives him the courage to undertake this impossible task, is that he has actually explored the sciences and their transformations where his predecessors saw only Science, singular, and double-click communication. In his opinion, there has never been, till now, any credible comparison between the scientific forms and the religious forms of utterance. The stage has always been taken by communication. Well, the latter has only ridiculed the forms of convey-ance that were supposed to pay their way by immense and perilous transformations. And, in actual fact, in contrast to a form of truth that travels without paying, all the other forms of truth appear crude and falsifying, since they toil and sweat along stony paths, like real yokels, much like the little donkey loaded with wood that a high-speed train whistles past.

But what happens if we stop measuring them by the standard of double-click communication and compare these two modes of travel among themselves: the one used by science, involving transformation and information, and the one used by religion, involving transformation and translation? What place does religious speech take once we no longer compare it with Science, but with the sciences that the author has been studying for twenty-five years? In which new ecology can these two forms of practice deploy themselves and take their distance? He claims to be one of the only people who can talk about religion again because he remains just as agnostic when it comes to Science as he is when it comes to belief. Most other people (if they give a rat's arse about the subject) hope to extend Science over religion's territory through an offensive apologetics, or to protect religion's territory from Science through a defensive apologetics. He – and only he? – doesn't think there is any territory to extend because the sciences don't take over the world with red or green patches, like empires on geography maps; they lodge themselves in the world quite differently: along narrow conduits that they drill through from the inside, digesting them like termites. On the other hand, he knows very well that the blind faith in Science felt by the naively trusting exercises such a powerful hold over people's minds that he doesn't have a chance of being heard. This is why, without a mandate, without authority, he stumbles on, moving abruptly, like any cyclothymic, from megalomania to 'micromania'. A voice crying in the wilderness.

Happily, we all have daily experience of ways of talking that double-click communication doesn't govern. Imagine a lover who answered the question 'Do you love me?' with this sentence: 'Yes, but you already know that, I told you so last year.' (We might even imagine he recorded this memorable sentence on a tape recorder and that, as his only answer, he's happy just to press the *replay* button to produce the indisputable proof that he truly loves . . .). You'd be hard pressed to find more decisive evidence that he has stopped loving in earnest. He has taken the request for love as a request for information, as though he'd decided to carve out a path through space-time and, through the intermediary of a document, a map, to return to the distant territory of the day he officially declared his love. From the quality of his answer, any impartial observer would understand that the lover hasn't understood a thing. The fact is his girlfriend didn't ask him if he *had* loved her, but if he loves her *now*. That is her request, her entreaty, that is his challenge.

Now, it may well be that the lover brings off the linguistic act required of him, and by way of an answer utters a sentence that resembles word for word the one he did indeed say a year earlier. If we compared the two recordings, we wouldn't detect any difference in form: the information content, to talk as computer scientists do, would be zero. Conversely, the lover might manage to express the same love, not through repetition of the formula now, but through something quite different that bears no relationship of *resemblance* to the sentence he is being asked to recapture: a gesture, an act of kindness,

25

a look, a joke, a quivering of the glottis. In both cases, the relationship is no longer the one a map has with a territory across the stream of transformations that maintain a constant. Either it dissociates sentences that resemble each other word for word but mean quite different things through the movement that captures them, or it makes diverse expressions synonymous through word forms that don't in any way resemble each other. As soon as we talk of love, the letter and the spirit part company.

And so it isn't the sentence itself that the woman will closely follow, or the resemblance or dissimilitude between the two instances, but the *tone*, the manner, the way in which he, her lover, will revive that old, worn-out theme. With admirable precision, exact to the second, she will detect if the old refrain has captured the new meaning she was waiting for, if it has renewed in an instant the love that her lover feels for her, or if the weariness and boredom of a liaison long over show through the worn-out vocables. No information is conveyed by the sentence and yet she, the woman who loves, feels transported, transformed, slightly shaken up, changed, rearranged, or not, or the opposite, alienated, flattened, forgotten, mothballed, humiliated. There are sentences uttered every day, then, whose main object is not to map out references but which seek to produce something else entirely: the *near* and the *far*, closeness or distance. Who hasn't had some experience of this?

How can we not feel that it would be fraudulent to judge this speech requirement solely in terms of undistorted communication? Clearly, a hint of a reference always clings to amorous talk; essential information is in fact provided on the inner state, the psychology and the sincerity of the interlocutors, just as, conversely, an offer of closeness or distance always circulates within the most rigorous information – there are people who are charmed even by the mechanical voice of a talking clock. But we need to heighten contrasts here, bring out what each regime of utterance – the scientific and the religious – specifically conveys, its specific wavelength, even if we later acknowledge interference and overtones. As overlapping as these utterances may be in everyday practice, their felicity conditions (as they say in the philosophy of language) remain incommensurable. Both regimes judge accurately and with merciless discernment the true and the false, but the fact is, they don't define the true and the false the same way. What one takes for a truth, the other takes for an outrageous deformation, and the other way round. We can't translate them, either, into some superior language that would give both their due, for their definition of what is meant by 'transformation', 'deformation', 'lie', 'truth', 'transfer', 'faithfulness', 'unfaithfulness' varies in terms of the regime of utterance, the key written at the start of the score (not to leave out the terms 'comparison', 'superior', and 'understanding', which also differ from one form to the other). This is why it is so hard to start talking again when the power of double-click communication reigns undivided: we no longer understand to what extent we don't understand each other.

Far from trying to cover up this distinction surreptitiously, it would be better if, on the contrary, we heightened it, explored it, familiarized ourselves with it in every possible way, for that's the only way not to scandalize when we have to draw from this difference between speech regimes its inevitable consequence: what we call religious speech *has no reference* – any more than amorous exchanges do. Of course, it has a server, in the old-fashioned sense of the term of one serving at mass; it does indeed register something essential; uttered judiciously, it is neither empty nor vain. It very definitely has some referent, then, in the ordinary sense of the term. But it doesn't have a referent in the precise sense of the term that the study of the sciences has allowed us to define: it does not distil information through a chain of graduated documents, each of which serves as material for formatting the next one. The thing is that, with these sentences, which are as mysterious as they are banal, we hope to get closer and not move further away. They don't provide any access. They don't teach anything about anything. They don't drive. They don't form holds we can get any kind of grip on. You *don't go anywhere* with them you don't travel anywhere by taking the vehicle, the intermediary, of religious utterances, words, texts, rituals. There is no subscriber at the number you dialled.

And just as well, since that's not what it's about. Nothing has made religious speech more inaudible, more unsayable than the ungodly habit of behaving as if it could follow the path of reference, just a bit less neatly, a bit less clearly, a bit less demonstrably. As if anyone needed to *add* to the conveyance of clear and distinct messages by conveying obscure and coded messages. As if the utterances differed only in the goal to be attained while being composed, basically, of the same materials, shaped for the same journeys along the same paths. As if we could add to the production of information that we can experiment with and verify by meandering through streams of references, by producing information about something *no one can* experiment with or verify; as if we could still talk about information or even pseudo-information when there is *no* meandering course guaranteed to allow us to preserve a constant throughout successive deformations. This is the sorry origin of belief, the belief we've decided to do without.

Taken in the sense of trust, everyone agrees, belief is as indispensable as the air we breathe. We definitely need to give credit if we want to exchange, live, think, speak. The agnostic, in this sense, would be an asocial, autistic lunatic. But, taken in the sense of a *demand for access that has been stripped of its practical means of acceding to anything at all*, belief is an artefact engendered by the conflict – also artificial – between Science and religion. In which case, nothing could be more indispensable than becoming agnostic. It's as if, to defend itself against the hold, judged to be deleterious, of Science, religion had tried to emulate it by going above and beyond, while sticking to the same vehicle. The superfluous burden of belief is disposed of as soon as the believer is faced with a choice: either you are looking for access to the far distant, and you give yourself the means of finding it by gradually introducing forms capable of gathering information; or you are not looking for access to the far distant but want to get closer to the person you are addressing, and then what you gather will never be information. Confusing the two amounts to making a mistake as complete as the mistake the lover makes when he misunderstands the question 'Do you love me?'

There is no intermediate solution, no rough and ready compromise.

Why does belief in belief make any revival of religious speech impossible? Because it leads thinking astray into a virtual world, one to which we 'could' have access 'if only' we had the means available to chains of information but of which belief actually remains forever deprived. It is this sleight of hand and nothing else that engenders the illusion of another world to which religious discourse, by some miraculous somersault, would provide exclusive access. People have even dared imagine a race, a competition, a sort of championship between informational speech and religious speech to see which of them went further, took us further. As if this hare and that tortoise could be pitted against each other on the same grounds – of speed and access to the far distant! And to rig the race, which was over before it even started, between the slow and steady march of the scholarly tortoise and the lightning bounds of the religious hare, they even came up with the assertion that the former was running in 'the merely material and visible world' while the latter was able to leap towards 'a spiritual and invisible world'. Never has religious speech been more led astray, insulted, perverted, never has G.'s name been spoken more falsely than when they claimed to have the means of using it to accede to another world *beyond* this world. There is no more beyond than there is belief *in* 'God', no 'spiritual' world coming on top of the 'material' world. It's just as pointless imagining 'limits' to scientific knowledge beyond which we'd need to resort to some other vehicle, one that's lighter, faster, more evanescent. There is no boundary to the travail of reference: wherever it can spread its net of documents, it strides confidently ahead. To believe that there exists another world, or that access to this world alone has borders, and Columns of Hercules exist that it would be sinful to go beyond, stems from confusion between the different speech acts.

There may well be a spiritual way of speaking *in* this world that differs drastically, in fact, from the conveyance of double-click information, but there is no 'spiritual world' in addition to the other one. Besides, if we forget about the pieties of Science and look closely at the sciences themselves – the true sciences, those that exist in all their beauty, in all their referential meander-ings, in all their outcomes and their conveyances of charts or models – we realize that they don't depict a world that's more material and more visible, duller and baser. You would have to have never had any hands-on experience of the length, precariousness, splendour and originality of the streams of references that allow an astronomer to accede to the confines of the Big Bang, an oceanographer to map the movement of tectonic plates, a mathematician to prove a theorem on number theory, or a historian to retrace a popular uprising no one knew about, to believe that the world left behind in the wake of the sciences was basely material and visible, objective and obstinate, simply and stupidly there. If we really want to keep the adjective, what could be more 'spiritual', on the contrary, than the worlds begotten by the meandering of the sciences? What, in any case, could be less *directly* visible? If we can't possibly talk about religion without twists and turns and preliminaries, how many contributions do we have to string together to utter sentences, whether true or false, about the tiniest microbe, the remotest star, the briefest interaction between particles, the most banal of economies? If there's one thing that is actually impossible, it's being able to accede immediately, without work and without cost, to scientific chains of reference. The ever-reliable sciences, too, only write straight with crooked lines.

Conversely, you have to have never measured the profound disappointment all religious speech brings – has to bring – in order to be truthful. Disappoint, above all, disappoint. It is precisely the utter lack of information conveyed by the panoply of religious expressions that provides a guarantee that we will never be able to use them to proceed to secrets superior to the secrets of the sciences, to loftier mysteries, more exalted spiritualities, less indecipherable gnoses. Do a test: compile a list of everything said by the angels in the Bible, despite supposedly being tasked 'with conveying messages', and you'll learn next to nothing about anything. The information content of those thousands of injunctions remains close to zero – unless they're turned into clues guiding the erudite labours of linguists, archaeologists or specialists in angelology. This is because angels do not convey messages; they change those they address. What they transfer is not an information *content*, but a new *container*. They don't bring maps offering some hold to beings starved of knowledge – they transform their interlocutors. What they convey are not telegrams but persons. How many bits can be carried by advice such as 'Believe!', 'Watch out, be ready', 'It's you we're speaking to', 'Look out!', '*Ave*', "He's not here'? The first word of any telephone exchange, 'Hello', what linguists call the phatic function, says as much: 'Communication is established'; 'You're wanted on the phone.'

It's an angel of the sort that passes in the sentence where the woman asks her lover to declare his love again today – even if the poor fool has made a translation mistake and has only heard a question asking him to reconnect, via a bridge of reference, to an event that occurred twelve months ago. Yes, of course, we can and must distinguish between messages that speak in order to provide information about the world and those that speak in order to change the world's inhabitants, but we can't confuse this necessary distinction with information about that world, on the one hand, and, on the other, with (obscure, mysterious, lost, encrypted) information about an 'other' world. There is no aspiration to the beyond that is of religious inspiration. Either it's information and it leads to various worlds – the only ones that exist; or it isn't information, and it *leads* nowhere – but it can perform plenty of other miracles. There is no in-between.

We have to go through this fundamental disappointment: religion leads nowhere. It is the absolute opposite of social or sociologizing explanations that think they've explained the need for religion as a bid to fill a world that's too empty or, conversely, according to the chosen metaphor, as a means of carving out a bit of transcendence in a world that's too full. As if frustrated souls had to fill up the holes in existence with the spectacle of higher truths; as if the vacuity of a merely material, mercantile world demanded extra soul to bring a bit of consolation to our vain existences;

33

as if we had to paint the sky in cheery colours to make the greyness of daily existence a bit more bearable; as if we had to quell the anguish of death with the evocation of ectoplasms leading a better life in a world hereafter. Well, it's exactly the opposite: no question will be resolved, no mystery revealed, no sin absolved, no prayer answered, no loss consoled. (Why speak at all, then?) It's by no means a matter of quelling, carving out, or filling up. 'He is risen; he is not here: behold the place where they laid him' [Mark 16:6]. No sign will be given. No answer to the 'great questions of existence'. (So why talk about these stale old notions again?) The world is not low enough for us to need to raise it. It's riddled with enough transcendencies for us not to add anything whatever to ennoble it; quite full enough for us not to need to fill it up; quite aired enough for us not to need to empty it. (What is the religious if it doesn't lead to the hereafter anymore?) Happily, by depriving ourselves of the other world, we don't in fact deprive ourselves of much, since all that it amounted to was confusion about the possibility of going further, faster, higher than the patient, meticulous and positive work of reference. In so disappointing, religion doesn't cut off the branch it is sitting on since there is no branch and it is firmly set up elsewhere, as we all are, in the world known to the sciences and inhabited by common sense. To have a chance of talking precisely about religion, you have first of all to love the sciences with all your might, with all your heart, with all your soul, and respect the worlds they leave in their wakes.

There is no other world, but there are several ways of living in this one and several ways, too, of knowing it.

A perverse taste for mysteries

For any religious spirit, this version of the spiritual as being lifted up gradually to another realm, one to which we might have access via expressions that preserve the form of reference without having all its properties, must be horrifying. There may well be people who are truly spiritual, but the test guaranteed to sort them from the falsely spiritual is to see whether they take you 'upwards', by trying to compete with the paths of information using other means, or whether, on the contrary, they gradually take you down into linguistic acts that transform interlocutors, without in any way diminishing their thirst for knowledge. If they claim to quell your *libido sciendi*, reveal secrets to you, initiate you into mysteries, lift you up to sublime spheres, then steer clear of them; but stick like glue to those that help you retrieve the movement of those words that don't give access, don't take you anywhere and especially not further or higher, but transform you – you – right now, the very moment they address you. It would be better still to avoid all spirituality altogether, or rather, to put it less provocatively, to wean ourselves for a few years, a few decades, off the habit, too quickly acquired, that made us link religion and altitude. What if we stopped turning our eyes heavenward, sighing, every time someone uttered the word religion? Yes, we could go on a kind of retreat, take a sabbatical, have a jubilee, during which we'd ban anything spiritual, and wipe out the debts and deficits of translation. A sort of moratorium, of letting the land lie fallow, to unlearn these conditioned reflexes that pointlessly paralyse religious speech.

Why has it become so hard to mark the difference between what allows access to the distant – reference – and what allows us to transform someone distant into someone close – conversion? It's because of the notion of 'mystery' that belief in belief has clouded. It is perfectly true that the misunderstanding evident between the woman's question to her lover and her thick-headed partner's answer remains hard to define, true also that you can't directly grasp the question without testing it in a phrase that has the same effect as a conversion, true lastly that no by-the-book demonstration would make a person who's no longer in love understand the gesture he should have made, the spirit that should have prompted him to answer. But if that gesture remains hard to determine, there's nothing incomprehensible or ineffable about it even so. Besides, the stream of effects that allows us, in the real practice of the sciences, to connect a map to a territory, and to come and go from one to the other, offers our intellect a mystery every bit as profound. We'd stray off track in earnest if we pitted the depths of love against the superficiality of information. The two regimes of utterance presuppose dizzying transformations between words and things. It is no easier to understand how a constant is maintained intact through a chain of reference than it is to follow the mechanism by means of which the sound of words said properly allows the distance that separated two lovers to be eliminated. Only the myth of double-click communication allows us to act as if we could do away with all mediation by acceding directly, through sheer transparency, to a shift that would not come at the cost of some distortion. And so, despite the very real difficulties that scientific or religious work attests to, the adjective 'mysterious', in both uses, doesn't refer to anything obscure, inaccessible or unsayable: only to a gesture you have to have repeated, a savoir-faire you really need to practise a long while if you want to live well, if you don't want to lose either the near or the far. 'Mysterious' doesn't refer to what is hidden, obscure or coded, but to what is risky, clever and well done.

Alas, the translation arrears have mounted so high that people have even gone as far as hocking the very notion of mystery by swapping the real difficulties for false depths. They've preserved the capacity of scholarly utterances to lead us towards the distant, but only by ripping out all the subtle mechanisms by means of which scholars are accustomed to verifying that what they say, at every stage, does indeed refer to something. Once this forgery has been performed, all that are left are questions that are awkward, preposterous and dishonest, like the question that common sense has often seen as forming the core of religion while it has become just one more impiety today: when you are asked the question 'Do you belief *in* God?' and you answer 'Yes, I believe *in* God', you pretend to believe that the exchange is just like this other one: 'Do you believe in global warming?' 'Yes, because of recent results which show that in the last decade we've seen the eight hottest years since temperature began to be measured in a viable and standardized way by a chain of meteorological stations spread throughout the globe.' The only problem is that, although the second question is perfectly formulated, the first is *misplaced*. For belief 'in God', we don't have the network of instruments, laboratories and satellites that would allow us to obtain, compile and model the data we have at our disposal for the climate. And don't anyone try and save face and say that the incompleteness of the referential act in the first exchange is due to the opposition between the visible and the invisible, for global warming is exactly as invisible to the naked eye, to the eye not equipped by the sciences, as this 'God' to whom we claim to accede by an act of knowledge that some kind of strange sabotage has left hanging for all time. This is one of the touchstones for distinguishing a real mystery from a false mystery: in the first exchange, you maintain the desire for reference, but are careful not to offer a feasible path for taking it to its logical conclusion. The question only makes you want to race to the information path, it puts you in the starting blocks, but you stumble before you even start since, in these matters, you don't have any proof at your disposal that would allow you to finish the work and produce verifiable information. We've laughed a bit too hard at the good Gagarin, the first anti-cleric to travel in space, because he used to say that, not having spotted 'God' from the tiny porthole of his cramped cabin, he had sufficiently proved his non-existence. Gagarin's proof was perfect, actually, since it corresponded precisely to the requirement of visibility of scientific tools. In the sky, there is no 'God'.

It is at this precise point that the devil ambushes us, offering our covetous eyes the grandiose perspective of a hell paved with good intentions. 'What if the difficulty in answering the question', he whispers, 'stemmed from the fact that these lofty and profound matters elude reference altogether; if you didn't need to add invisible and inaccessible things to visible and accessible things; if they formed mysteries that you really shouldn't try to go into more deeply; if it was actually impious to want to get to the bottom of them?' The temptation is strong, we can well understand, to preserve the movement of reference, the arrow, but also then to say, well, since we're not interfering with anything and haven't acceded to the distant, we've obviously nailed some subtle object impossible to get a grip on. This is because the devil has more than one trick in his bag and can even, by a truly admirable bit of showmanship, feign humility: 'Who are you to try and see through these mysteries? Bow your proud head and understand at least that you can't understand them.' And so from insinuation to provocation, from feigning to temptation, you wind up accepting that religion may indeed be about unfathomable mysteries ... The jig's up. These mysteries are beyond us, so let's pretend to organize them. And that's so very comfortable, it makes so very many things easier: there is nothing left to revive, rethink, renew. You can let yourself go on painlessly deepening the translation deficit; whenever the time lag makes words incomprehensible, you can just say that they are actually incomprehensible because they *have to* be, because what we're dealing with are profound mysteries – whereas you've simply forgotten to press the playback button. How can we resist such a drug? We even go as far as hitting rock bottom, that ultimate stage of intoxication where the devil, faced with the dizzying mass of false mysteries, manages to trick the finest minds into uttering this monstrous sentence: '*Credo quia absurdum*', 'I believe *because* it is absurd.' And this sentence will be celebrated as a marvellous new mystery even though it merely attests to a cowardly abandonment, the fact of our sinking further and further into decline: 'What courage,' they'll say, 'what faith the man who utters such desperate words must have, as he hangs on grimly to life!' Yes, he will indeed need courage to withstand the flames of hell that now surround him on all sides, a hell into which he suddenly plunged when he thought he was going straight to paradise in a perilous double somersault. This is where subscribing too quickly to the easy option of mysteries gets you. This is the conflagration where those who believe in belief end up.

Instead of trying to answer the question 'Do you believe *in* something?' he should have refused to answer, with a polite apology: 'Sorry, but the question isn't put very well, isn't framed very well' or, more brutally: 'Ask a stupid question, get a stupid answer.' The request could not, in fact, lead anywhere. Or rather, it actually tried to lead somewhere, to accede to a distant territory where they then claimed to be able to decide if that particular being, 'God', was to be found or not. And naturally, as luck would have it, as they were closing the discussion, they explained to us that there was no means, no tool, no intermediary to determine such a thing. The utterance was presented as having a truth value that could be calculated by a yes or a no, by a p and a q, but wound up without any truth value at all.

Well, we should have resorted to a very different language game: 'Put me a question that isn't trying to lead anywhere, but allows us to forge someone anew.' For instance, a question that, instead of taking the form of 'Do you believe in global warming?', goes more like this: 'Do you love me?' Once we rely on this new template, we immediately discover we no longer have any right, in such a speech regime, to be obscure. Whereas the previous questions left room for mystery, this one must be understood at the outset, otherwise it will have *no effect* on the person it's supposed to change, convert, transform. The woman would have played a quite perverse role if she had concealed her demand for love in such overblown words that her lover couldn't understand either the demand or the challenge. The sin would then have passed from him, in refusing to understand the injunction, to her, in deliberately rigging the test, making it impossible for him to pass the final exam. Conversion speech that is incomprehensible is dishonest, impious speech. Adding the false scandal of a false mystery to the enormous difficulty of the required transformation – this may well be the ultimate sin in matters of religion. Unless the interrogation bravely does its work of reference, struggles hard to convey information just as the scholarly tortoise does – but then it would need to be given the means to travel and to accede to the distant, to say nothing of getting its fill of porkies . . . For pity's sake, don't ask the tortoise 'to prove the existence of God'; if it comes back empty-handed, don't talk about mystery; if no one understands your gobbledegook, don't sing the praises of the absurdity essential to faith. I may fail to be clear, but, in any event, I won't try and hide behind the obscurity of mysteries.

There is no way out: if you want to convert anew, you have to be as clear as day (which is, of course, impossible, since we can never talk directly about what's involved . . .). When the Scriptures say that, at Pentecost, everyone understood the glad tidings, the revival of the ancient message, the renewal of a doctrine that had gone stale till then – in short, the Gospel *in its own language* – we can well grasp the felicity conditions for this speech act on the part of the apostles. Instead of having to translate the Phrygian or Parthian into the tongue of the Galileans, instead of having to shrug off their ethnicity and turn their eyes towards another, exotic world, instead of painfully removing a series of artificial obstacles placed in the way of comprehension, all those diverse peoples found themselves gripped from the word go by this overwhelming demand: no other difficulty was being proposed to them than the difficulty, great enough in fact, of converting. From this real mystery of the transformation of interlocutors on hearing the message, no false mystery came to divert them by luring them with, say, the mirage of possible access to the distant. Feeling the full brunt of a saving arrow within the narrow framework of their language, of their ethnicity, of their times, they had nowhere to run – unless, say the Scriptures, an 'abuse of sweet wine' didn't turn their heads . . . Alas, what should we call this *anti*-Pentecost that today forces all the peoples scattered over the earth *not* to understand, each in his own tongue, the *same* message, now indecipherable: it conceals its address so completely that whenever we hear it, we feel obliged to direct our thoughts to another world and another time, over there, to Jerusalem, to Rome, or up there in the sky – places which, for want of an access ramp, remain forever unattributable? If everyone once understood the same message in their own tongue at Pentecost through the intercession of the Holy Spirit, what should we name this anti-Paraclete who has scrambled the glad tidings so completely that everyone

42

manages – o unpardonable crime! – not to understand this incredibly simple transformation anymore, now that it has become *equally* foreign to all tongues, to all peoples, to all times? How can we not cry bitter tears before this reversal of the figures of the universal, of the forms of catholicity?

If we want to get the translation machine up and running again, if we want to understand how a message can remain 'the same' across translations that make it unrecognizable, we need to distinguish between the different senses of that little word. This is because you can't mix universals up at your pleasure. Either you hope to designate a similarity produced by *standardization*, or to designate a similarity produced by *retrospective understanding*. Either you are looking for what is stable across space and time, or you change the way you put space and time together. Here again, you have to choose.

Even though the first form is scarcely any more familiar than the second, to the extent that it depends on obscure work as carefully concealed from view as the hard labour of the sciences, it's easier to grasp, since it hasn't suffered as much from contrast with double-click communication. Thanks to the meticulous work of *metrology* and the endless scruples of metrologists, it is now possible everywhere to foster the same reference standards that facilitate the search for constants and allow the establishment, followed by the maintenance, of chains of reference. There is no map without the standard metre, no weather report without degrees Celsius and millibars, no classification of wind force without the Beaufort Scale, no measurement of living standards without the shopping basket, no computers without the running of atomic clocks in pico-seconds, no calculation of tonnage without the platinum kilo in the Sèvres Pavillon, which France (the home of metrology as well as elder daughter of the Church) keeps in a vault buried in the ground, away from prying eyes.

Thanks to this slow, onerous and costly maintenance of standards, we are no longer amazed to see the Medes and the Basques, the Mesopotamians and the Californians making use of the same figures, the same letters, the same measurements, the same conventions. This is because, across all times and all places, and at great expense, laboratories of reference and international institutions maintain the same constant *constants*. All double-click communication has to do after that is erase the work of the metrologists and the metrology networks so it can then wheel in a universal that would cost nothing, that wouldn't need any tool, or team, or institution. That way it can put its precious stamp of indisputable universality on Science. And rehash this cliché of scholarly claptrap: 'At equal pressure, water, as everyone knows, boils everywhere and always at 100 degrees.' Yes, but only on condition of leaving out the work of standardization essential for inter-laboratory comparison of measurements of temperature and pressure . . . The channels are indeed narrow that allow this solemn assertion, this metrological habit, to circulate like a universal, like obvious fact.

That is all very well, fascinating, useful, profitable, indispensable, reassuring, but it is clearly not the extension of such a yardstick that so filled with enthusiasm the peoples gathered together outside the house of the

44

Cenacle, on that miraculous day of the Pentecost. The word 'same', in the expression 'retrospective understanding of the same message', did not then have the character of a standard distributed everywhere and, basically, foreign everywhere, like the Greenwich Meridian or the standard metre. It wasn't one of those convenient conventions that allowed people to organize the maintenance of information across a stream of perilous transformations, through chains of witnesses, templates and signposts. Whether I'm Persian or Kabyl, Icelandic or Bororo, my GPS sensor allows me to know where I am anywhere thanks to the same pinpointing of latitude and longitude. But it is not that kind of conveyance, that kind of faithfulness or exactitude, truth or feasibility that I follow when I seek to understand what 'hearing the same glad tidings in my own tongue' might mean. Information networks have their grandeur, their importance, their efficacy, their spirituality, if you like, but in the end they don't amount to a Pentecost. And don't let anyone claim that all the Day of the Feast of Weeks involves is simple 'localization' as when, with a click of the mouse on my laptop computer, I can cause the keyboard to swing from Chinese to Arabic, or from English to Quebecois. Adjusting the standards to all concrete situations requires rules for combining solutions established for good and this implies yardsticks that are even more general, even more abstract, even more conventional. No, it was not some 'local adjustment' to their 'ethnic particularities' that was able to shake up those rough and tumble visitors who'd come to sacrifice on the Temple esplanade. The apostles had not 'adapted' their message to all those barbaric languages

45

trooping past. It had nothing to do with standardization or localization. On that blessed day, people were struck by a different form of progressive universalization: they were finally being spoken to in their own language, and the words spoken called on them to be part once again of the same people, to be faithful once again to the same tradition, to be trustees of the same message whose meaning was at last understood and made real.

Can we produce this kind of emotional shock ever again? Have we once and for all lost the trade secret for manufacturing those tongues of fire that floated over the heads of the apostles and inspired them to talk in all the tongues of the world? Maybe not, even though the idea of transparent and permanent, universal and stable communication has made that secret so foreign to our public ways of speaking that religion appears as impossible to refloat as the wreck of the *Titanic*, eaten into by rust. How can we save religion? By going back yet again to the utterly humdrum, utterly banal example of the lovers' dialogue.

Let's suppose that the man understood his lover's injunction perfectly well, that he has groped around clumsily for the right words to restate his love and found them. How are they both, after that, going to go about relinking these new words to their initial avowal? They're going to say that it's the 'same' love that makes them close again, after a phase of distance. But, naturally, this 'same' is in no way of the nature of a substance preserved intact over time, such as a gold coin forgotten under a mattress that you might come across happily years later. Focusing on such a form of the 'same', on such stability over time and space, is exactly the temptation the man needed to avoid in order wisely to utter the sentence that renewed their relationship. Whereas such a reaction would have been perfectly right if he had had to answer a demand for positioning, for information, for reference – if he'd been asked, for instance, to list his pension points, meandering along a chain of transformations, looking for figures that have remained intact across sundry account statements. Once they are close again, then, the reunited lovers can rightly say they've *got back* the 'same love', everlasting over time, even though they know perfectly well that everything has changed, themselves and the times with them.

So, there is indeed – we've all had daily, fleeting, fragile, subtle experience of this – a particular way, absolutely unique, of fostering some of the 'same', the identical, the continuous, even though it doesn't rely on maintaining a substance intact over time and space. This particular universal is so unlike the other kind that, far from coming down, stable, from the past to the present, it takes off from the present and goes back to the past, changing and deepening the past's foundation. So much so that, the more time passes, the more the point of departure swells with the future. What happens after that allows the beginning to be the beginning of something. The start depends on the sequel. The father depends on the son. This reversal of the usual figures of time is something the lovers fully feel, since they can say without lying that the love that moves them now as though it had always existed is infinitely stronger, deeper and more solid, and that it brings them closer together than when they started out. To such a point that it gives them the amazing feeling that it is finally only now, *for the first time*, that they understand what has happened to them *always*. Yes, as you know very well, 'it's always the first time' – otherwise you don't love each other anymore.

What relationship might exist between this retrospective understanding of their love on the part of the lovers, which is certainly an overwhelming experience but one that's individual, private, almost psychological, and this universal-in-motion that is the religious utterance which mobilizes, which is supposed to mobilize, the masses with their very different dialects? The lifeline, the flimsy hoisting sling of love is pretty feeble, I know, but it's the only way I can think of to try and refloat that grounded wreck, to haul it little by little out of the deep, and once again mull over the sinking of religion. For in the end, it is this by now foreign way of producing unity, unification, the universal, and not the way of standardization, that seems to have converted the peoples gathered for the Feast of Pentecost, according to the narrative we find in the Acts of the Apostles.

Those words, heard a thousand times, which we'd become accustomed to, and which distanced us from each other, suddenly ring out afresh as though for *the first time*, to the point of feeling new to us, even though all they do is repeat the same, never-ending refrain, just as the lover's words do. And we form anew something very like a people, since, with everyone hearing the same thing in his own language, we once again feel close to each other – no! a lot closer than we've ever been, as if we were finally, for the first time, deepening that same feeling of belonging. 'Ah!' we cry, stunned, 'so these were the words we used to say without even thinking!

The undue mixing of universals

That our fathers used to recite without our understanding what they meant! So this is the meaning of all those rituals we used to perform automatically! These neighbours, with their strange customs, actually turn out to be our brothers, in spite of all this diversity, this Babel of scattered tongues? How obtuse we were', we say, smacking ourselves in the head, 'not to better understand the injunction that was being addressed to us!' So, there really exist such miraculous words, then, that produce those who say them at the same time as those who hear them, *gathering them together into a newly convened people* united by the same message *finally made real?* So, the banal experience of the two lovers resembles in form, regime and tone the experience of whole nations? So, despite the dictatorship of transparent communication, we kept the capacity for speech intact, right up to our own day – speech itself also capable, as on the first day – better than on the first day – of assembling similar people together, dumbfounded as they might be at having strayed so long without realizing that what they were telling each other every morning dispassionately could once more reunite them. Can't you feel the wreck stirring, as though it had broken free of the bottom, as though it was finally about to reappear on the surface?

But it sinks back down again immediately, all hoisting slings having snapped, and plunges even more deeply into the submarine sludge for, having only just differentiated between them, we confuse the two universals – the inalterable standard and retrospective understanding – and turn the mix into an amorphous monster. We begin to assume that behind every story, regardless of its twists and turns, there is a unique substance, impervious

49

to change, which, remaining always what it was on the first day, would explain the diversity of acts of conversion. As if being converted came down to plugging into this intangible thing so as to retrieve the consoling certainty of absolute immobility, beyond history. This is how they fashioned most of the figures of the old 'God' – the thing that, thanks to weariness and compromise, they gave up translating as 'ordinary, everyday framework'. That constant universal 'God', that substantial 'God', that standard 'God', is on this account – how can I say this without wounding? – a mere artefact, a mere pseudo-scientific proposition, deprived of the practical means of laying out scientific proofs of his existence. A scholarly hope castrated – *libido sciendi interrupta*.

So many admirable texts have been written explaining Pentecost as the encounter of poor human beings with that intangible substance, that constant maintained identical throughout the vicissitudes of history, that we tremble to have thus to blaspheme. But to be faithful you have to be unfaithful, to retrieve the sense you have to abandon the letter, to retranslate, you have to dare to sacrifice the old translation; to betray/translate afresh, you have to not hesitate (but I do I hesitate and tremble!) to translate/betray afresh. This is because what I most want not to do is to confuse G. with some sophisticated GPS. Otherwise I'll need to be shown the network of satellites and atomic clocks, receptors and international conventions that allows us to receive him everywhere, 'loud and clear', identical and miraculously co-ordinated. If we have to keep these two forms of universalization, these two regimes of catholicity (there are others, of course, but only these two interest us for

50

the moment) as a precious asset, we must above all not merge them into a single regime, which would give us neither the advantages of the one nor the charms of the other. Contrary to this confusion, we have to say that there is no relationship between 'the same', as it is produced at great cost by maintenance of constants thanks to metrology, and 'the same' as it is produced by sacrifice through the revival, always recommenced, always deepened, always broadened, of a decisive message that transforms forever the lives of those who then recognize themselves instantly as members of the same people. Two different universals clearly, both capable of spreading gradually, both capable of producing unity and agreement, both essential to a civilized life, but which we have to maintain as incommensurable at the risk of impiety.

To counter the obsession with a universal constant that no effective metrology could enable us to back up, we need to go deeper still into the lovers' experience. If they were to speak about their love as a G., they would be very careful not to turn it into an inalterable substance the same as it ever was beneath the variety of its attributes, for they know very well that you can't ever actually rely on it once and for all. On the contrary, one wrong word and suddenly there's distance, maybe even a crisis. What lovers call their love, that love capable of lasting and growing deeper, always materializes for them in the fragility of a risky speech act that forces them to keep on raising the stakes. Depending on how they speak to one other, they either find themselves as distant as strangers or closer than they've ever been. Who among us has lived such an oblivious or sorry life as not to have had the devastating dual experience of a crisis in love? That one word too many that transforms lovers into enemies who don't see how they could have lived so long in such stifling intimacy; that one word too many that transforms enemies into lovers who don't see how they could have starved themselves of oxygen so long by staying at such a distance. In a flash, they swing from one existence to the other, no matter how drastically different these are. This particular mystery is on a par with all the rest. In the wake of the lovers, I get closer, stammering, to a form of G. that depends on speech, on the rightness of the utterance, yes, on the tone, on how it's said. An infinitely fragile form whose evocation I'm keenly aware can be bungled. How can that name ever be said without striking a false note?

And yet, all the richness of the crisis in love stems from the fact that it has preserved our experience of the fragility of utterance for us. It prepares us and trains us in the radical transformation that even affects the way time passes, the linking and articulation of time. In effect, when 'you are apart', all the moments of being apart bind together to form an inexorable fate, a definitive essence, a *fatum*: '*Really*, we just weren't made for each other.' Then, the moments of closeness seem like folly; time starts flowing *from the past to the present*, as though you'd squandered a capital made up of love. But as soon as the lovers are close again, all the moments of being apart seem like moments of incomprehensible madness to them: the episodes of closeness are regrouped to form quite a different story, which flows back from that first time today to all the other times, going back, through a retroactive movement, *from the present to the*

52

past, to the *first* first time. As though they'd just discovered an inexhaustible capital that enriched the past as much as it ensured the future. Haven't you ever felt that sudden conversion that even changes the course of time? And haven't you experienced its constant instability, to the point where anyone emerging from a crisis in love, and counting like a banker on a fat capital of accrued history, hopes to hang on to this monument of affection but finds himself, a second later, in the same temporal misery, the same stifling situation that he thought he'd got out of for good? He'd relied on the guarantee of an exemplary love that was stable and assured; and now everything has vanished into thin air, just like in those stories where gold crowns are transformed, by the wave of a magic wand, into puddles of water.

If they spoke of their love as of a G., the lovers would therefore be very careful not turn it into capital that's likely to be exhausted bit by bit, drop by drop; they would not turn it into an incorruptible substance, indifferent to the speech acts, good or bad, through which they renew their faith in each other on a daily basis. The ridiculous idea would never occur to them to take the risk, fragility or precariousness out of their love, *its dependence on speech, right or wrong*, that dizzying way of always skirting an abyss into which their affair, however long it may have been going on, risks toppling at any moment in a radically opposite experience of time. That's the real truth value of the utterances they treasure, the real calculation they indulge in, the true yes or no that gauges the quality of their existence. If they really wanted to fashion a G. that they could call 'their love' – and how many hours do lovers not spend talking about this particular divinity, this power that keeps them both in suspense, on alert? – they'd want to give it the properties of urgency and risk; they'd behave in such a way that it crops up in what they say, always; they would keep it verging on crisis, ever threatened with incompleteness, ever sensitive to that sudden reversal in the passage of time. There are so many characteristics to render in paintings, in images, in the sacred story of their G., that they'd need to have long developed a habit, they'd need to have infinite scruples and to take endless care to be really sure of having listed all its attributes and registered all its graces. They would joyfully start the task all over again if they noticed they'd left this or that feature out, for every day the very difficulty of talking about these things – so ordinary, but so subtle, so different above all from the work, also admirable, of reference and of access to the distant – would oblige them to get back down to work on talk of their G. Why not try to talk once more about a divinity made in the image and the likeness of theirs?

When I make a list of the set of felicity conditions we've run through up to this point by sticking to the example of the lovers' crisis – the only language game to still more or less elude the empire of communication – how can I help but feel discouraged?

Words that redress must be comprehensible, that's the first condition; they must be said in the language of the person they are addressed to, without adding any superfluous difficulty of translation. As the risk of stumbling is already great, it would be madness, in distinguishing what creates distance from what creates closeness, to add another stumbling block.

54

Second condition: these formal speeches must be directed to the present situation, to us, here and now, without diverting our attention, without rehashing old grievances, without claiming to settle scores over some old debt. It's the present that's at issue, not the past.

Third felicity condition: these injunctions must at no time try to seek a compromise with sentences full of information that might lead, through the intermediary of a chain of reference, to access to the distant – otherwise, we need to switch to some other type of conversation where we can get down to talking passionately about the weather, about global warming and the Big Bang. But then, let's give ourselves the wherewithal to go the whole hog: no rough and ready compromise between words of conversion and words of information, between creating closeness and seeking the distant.

Fourth condition: the words that give life must have *an effect*, otherwise we say them falsely. This effect can only be the recapturing, at that precise moment, of that lost love, the fragile and temporary redressing – which nonetheless in that moment seems to be definitive and salutary – of time. Whereas time was falling heavily from the past and crushing the present (the dead had the living in its grip), now it's lighter, springing up out of the present to revive the past and open up the future (the living has the dead in its grip).

Which allows us to fulfil the final condition: a unity, an identity, a union or a people (in the lovers' case, a micro-people) finds itself reformed.

Trawl through the rich repertoire of your lovers' crises and check whether I've made a complete enough inventory of these felicity conditions. Doesn't this initial list allow us to hear what's at issue when someone asks: 'Do you love me?' Doesn't it allow us to understand why it would be unthinkable to retort with a loud, exasperated sigh: 'Of course I do, I've told you a hundred times' – guaranteed proof that the speaker no longer loves?

If I now use the model provided by the language game of love to draw up a list of the *infelicity* conditions in the matter of religion, I see they're a lot easier and consequently more frequently fulfilled.

First condition: the words that were supposed to give life are said in a foreign language addressed to people remote from us in history, space and culture – so much so that an infinite period of time would be needed to translate them into the present tense, well before we even begin to grasp the injunction they once bore.

Second condition: even if we could translate them, we wouldn't understand them, for they are no longer addressed to us, here and now, but to those, down there, in very ancient times. For those perfect strangers, they must have had a miraculous power but for us, who are no longer in their sandals, they feel like so much ranting, ridiculous pomposity, crazy make-believe.

Third calamitous condition: to rate them even a tiny bit seriously, we could grope our way along the meandering paths of the sciences, establish bridges and proofs, line up instruments and documents that would allow us to reconnect in thought with those distant times, those strange peoples, those bizarre expressions. But then we'd have to pay the high price of exegesis, of archaeology and history. In short, we'd have to accept the constraints of erudition, at the same time as those certainties. Well, we most often stop half-way, inventing all sorts of unconvincing compromises between access words and words of salvation, without managing to benefit from the advantages either offer.

Fourth infelicity condition: the words don't have the slightest effect; mediocre, they slide off our lives like rain on a windscreen. Because of this impotence, all they do is add to the gaudy shambles of tradition a new hotchpotch of myths and stories that further increase the stifling weight of the past. Unless we resign ourselves to aestheticizing these rites and anecdotes by finding memorable, amusing or touching what was for others, for our fathers and mothers, a question of life and death.

That is why, and it's the fifth condition, those who hear this torrent of insanities never form a holy nation but only an aggregate of strangers, even enemies, that nothing can bring together anymore.

Well, I've painted a faithful portrait of the ways religion most often appears today in the eyes of our contemporaries, haven't I? Hardly surprising my tongue feels so furry. With these five infelicity conditions, I've described incredibly precisely what is said every Sunday during the sermon, from up in the pulpits (I'm well aware no one 'mounts' the pulpit anymore), haven't I? I've accounted for my uneasiness, my confusion, and for your uneasiness, your embarrassment, when so many words of salvation ring out so falsely, haven't I?

And yet I go, I stay, I keep trying, yes, I persist, I even stick to my pew. That's because, as with the lovers' quarrel, about a quarter of a millimetre behind the infelicity conditions lie the felicity conditions, which remain intact; no! forever lost; yes! there, within easy reach; no! now inaccessible, indefinitely remote, untranslatable, squandered; yes! as fresh as the first day, better than the first day; no! no! without a hope of being revived since I'm one man alone, with no authority, with no right, with no imprimatur, with no mandate – I'm nothing, not even a believer (except it's not a matter of believing . . .). I still hesitate, as in the lovers' crisis, between two absolutely opposed forms of temporality, trust and faithfulness. Stop? Abandon everything? Restrict myself to the love of lovers? Be happy with the passion of scholars? Stop trying to float the wreck? I've said too much, I've taken too many risks: I have to go the whole hog, take stock of what it's possible and not possible to say. I'm launched. For every tree is known by its own fruit [Luke: 6:44], and if it doesn't bear any, let it be mercilessly burned down.

To get myself off the hook, I try to resort to flurries of 'mental reservations'. But what an ordeal! I have to replace what I say out loud – 'I believe in God, the Father Almighty' – with a translation that I have to do in my head quick smart . . . 'I am certain of the indisputable framework of ordinary existence, the power is not in question, and I know it's not about belief', and so on and so forth, till the end of the *Apostles' Creed* . . . But I don't keep at it long, my translation is too long, too slow, too convoluted; I can't quite catch up; I lose the thread; I'm forced to overlook unfathomable whoppers ('consubstantial', 'Virgin Mary', 'descended into hell', 'life everlasting') before we even get to the sermon, which will only add to these misunderstandings. It's such a torrent of ill-digested words that I can't quite reprocess them, recycle them, anymore; nothing for it, I'm out of synch; I'm overwhelmed, disgusted with myself for uttering so many truths grudgingly, and for not being able to spruce up so many untruths. So I give up hope since, even if I managed to formulate in my heart of hearts some transposition that satisfied me, *I wouldn't be able to share it*: it wouldn't be a form of life common to the people gathered around me; if they heard it said out loud, I'd scandalize my neighbours. Thus divided, at war with myself, when it comes to the kiss of peace, I become a monument of flesh dedicated to hypocrisy and blasphemy, and polluted by mental reservations like unto a whited sepulchre [Matthew 23:27].

And yet, I can't prevent myself from assuming that the people around me are having mental reservations, too, that, pedalling away like maniacs, they're forcing themselves to cover the space that separates these now untruthful words from words that have once again become for them perceptible and wise. People would be very surprised if some loudspeaker broadcast aloud from up under the nave what those present, at funerals, softly say in the place of the words 'life everlasting', 'hope', 'heaven'. But no one seems to help them any more than they do me, and we all hold our silence, unwittingly sharing the same discomfort. Right down to the clergy whom I, of course, suspect of performing adjustments and dodgy compromises, high-wire acrobatics, dizzying splits, just as I do, as their very unfaithful faithful do, as everyone does, to try and make distant, worn-out words sound current and close. All together we pray in the shadows of this rubbish tip that's as high as a hill, ready to come streaming over us, a mountain of debts, of translation arrears that paralyses our tongues and forces each one of us to mope as we sit on our chairs, not budging for fear that the whole thing will come tumbling down, protecting with a clumsy hand the DIY interior of a private religion, bric-à-brac that no longer has the capacity to assemble a people once again since no one dares anymore to give expression to it, out loud in public. It would seem that, after all this time, everyone has had to make 'his own religion', as they say, a little hotchpotch of half-lies and half-truths, lean as those pellets of bones owls regurgitate after they've eaten. It's worse, what's more, when, through some unfortunate innovation, a panel, a painting, a slogan, a speech, a ritual, one of us says out loud what he'd have been better off keeping to himself: artlessly, illiterately, without erudition, without culture, without tradition, without authority, the makeshift remains of words are then hung from the nave, their 'keeping up with the times' only increasing their terminal deathly pallor. Every one of us can think of examples in churches he has recently visited. In the face of certain drawings in felt-tip pen illustrating some holy word, put up with sticky-tape in the narthex by children learning their catechism, the stones themselves would sweat tears of blood. How do we get out of this one?

The solution of 'mental reservations' offers only an awful last resort. Another, more reasonable, solution would be to tidy the whole mess up, clean out the Augean stables, get rid of the most offensive rags, the most compromising anecdotes, the most kitsch hymns, in short, like rag-and-bone merchants in a garbage dump, sort out what can still be salvaged. In moments of extreme exasperation, great is the temptation to purify: let the whole set of religious rituals and beliefs be reduced to a restrained body of solid and truthful, clean and certified elements, and let the rest be tossed onto the purifying fire! This is religion within the limits of simple reason. Even if it has inflamed the greatest minds over the course of time, this desire for purity is just as unreasonable and just as impracticable as the perverse little game of 'mental reservations'. For where do you stop? Once you've started not sharing a speech regime anymore, nothing, absolutely nothing looks salvageable, for the same reason that the lovers, in the crisis of estrangement, can't find anything, not a phrase, not a gesture, not a moment, that can justify their past love: they were completely and utterly wrong about everything. You smash the hideous plaster statues? But why stop there? Why keep the altar stone? The ciborium? The stole? The host? The clergy? In this ordeal by fire, I've followed a very dear *abbé*, my uncle, every step of the way, and it's thanks to him that belief lost me along the way: I've seen him shake at every line of defence, as French officers did in June 1940, alarmed at seeing that no falling back stopped the rout, that the most solid-looking fortifications no longer offered any more resistance than a simple line drawn in the sand with a wet finger.

Naturally (!) you can always put out this devouring fire, this cheery auto-da-fé, in time, and rip some remnant out of the flames, but you will never have proof that it formed a core more resistant than the dross lying in the embers. One minute more and it, too, would've gone up in smoke. You burn the sacrament of confession? Why would the sacrament of baptism be

61

any more resistant? You part company with the pope? What good is keeping the bishops? You will never be able to justify why it was at this temperature and at this precise moment that the ordeal was called off. (How long do the lovers manage to hold out when, instead of getting out of the crisis by means of words that bring them close together, they decide to call off the dispute without explaining themselves; when they resign themselves to limiting their common life to the small circle of their habits? A month? A day? An hour?) Unless we revert to that other universal, the one produced by standardization, and manage, through convention, to define a common core, the lowest common denominator of religions, something so bland and so versatile that it could be spread throughout the world without shocking anyone. A 'moral ideal', a 'feeling of the infinite', a 'call to one's conscience', a 'richer inner life', 'access to the great all'? What a lot of poppycock that 'God' is! A simple portmanteau of morality – as if morality needed the support of religion. Thanks to such purification, we've got rid of the useless dross, but there's nothing left that would allow us to address ourselves in words that bring life to someone who, on hearing them, would find themselves transformed. In spite of, or because of, this work of reduction, sorting and purification, all the infelicity conditions find themselves joined together: the lowest common denominator of all religions, ripped from the specificities of time and place, is no longer addressed to me, right here, right now, but to anyone, anytime, anywhere. Yes, this is indeed the anti-Pentecost. By trying to save religion from the fire of criticism, we've transformed it into a bland universal that doesn't

62

even have the solid networks of physical constants to back it up. By trying to preserve something of this long religious experience in spite of everything, we've lost everything. As always, 'purity is indeed the vitriol of the soul', the supreme temptation that must be resisted.

But does this mean we should keep everything? Understand everything? Swallow everything? Accept everything? Yes, that's the only solution. I don't want to have to pick and choose; mental reservations exhaust me unnecessarily; heresy doesn't tempt me, nor does reform, or revolution, or any kind of upheaval. There is no dead wood in religious utterance, for everything in it is connected branches, experiment, trial, deep-rootedness, roots and rootlets. Either we understand what made these grow, and everything can be kept; or we don't, and everything can be burnt. If we have to revive the word once more, that means reviving every-thing, saving everything, clarifying everything, renewing everything, without abandoning a single sheep along the way; not a single bit of piety will be lost, not one vapid remark, religious trinket, holy souvenir, churchy knick-knack. I want to salvage all the treasure I was promised as my inheritance, for it to be mine for keeps – and *for me to be proud of it*. You have to have a big enough stomach, a generous enough mind, otherwise it isn't worth the trouble of embarking on this business, of pretending to try and talk about these things again. If it's just to save some rust-bucket of a ship from being wrecked, the game isn't worth the candle. There really are only two paths, the path of heresy – of selective choice – and the path of orthodoxy – the straight and narrow. Yes, but how do you walk straight? What are you to be faithful to once more and how? What might 'renewing everything without picking and choosing' mean – especially when we have to pick and choose, judge, repair, undo, reject, at the same time? No doubt about it, I find myself in the middle of the *torments* of religious speech.

Here he takes leave of his senses. Not a minute ago, he was floundering in mental reservations, trying to avoid falsely uttering so many untruths, and now he demands we swallow them whole without looking, with the faith of a gullible fool! He's even going as far as once again uttering the fatal words 'heresy' and 'orthodoxy', which have a strong whiff of the stake about them. Anyone has the right to hesitate, to be tormented, but surely not to this extent, not swinging like this from extreme unbelief to extreme credulity. Has he become as 'reactionary' as that?

Besides, he really must tell us one day what cowardly abandonment made him, too, believe, like all those of his generation, the *baby boomers*, in the inevitable disappearance of things religious. Why it seemed to him for so long that the modernization front was able to consign holy talk to oblivion, for the same reasons as the fuel stove and the oxcart. Yes, he must tell us a bit about why the 'progressives' so long shared the illusion that the opiate of the people was going to yield before the forces of emancipation and liberty – as if they themselves were not hooked on far more lethal drugs. They'll never admit it, but they were the ones who decided not to have their children baptized, to break with their own hands a thread that had remained unbroken for so many centuries, to deprive their children of belonging to the chosen people . . . Why? 'So they can choose for themselves later on!' O freedom, what crimes has this generation not committed in your name? The time will come when all these pickled babies, now *'grandpa boomers'*, are judged, being the only ones never to have known war yet who, in full peace, when nothing threatened them, wrecked with their own hands, one after the other, the tools for living that their parents had loaded them up with in their blessed childhood. Let them be revised in turn, too, these universal revisionists. They took full advantage of Sunday School as much as school, of the humanities as much as the sciences, of history as much as geography, of the state as much as politics, but what have they left their children? Autonomy. For it's in the name of holy freedom that they destroyed the institutions that brought them into existence. And what did they themselves bring forth? Stillborn babies. They're free all right, their offspring, horribly free, for the only thing they've inherited is freedom, whereas their unworthy parents were left those countless ties which they now realize, alas, too late, formed the very crux of autonomy. And the worst of it is that this whole generation is now ageing and querulously talking drivel and splitting hairs, they've started regretting the past, sighing over moral decline, the 'lowering of the bar', and going as far as hoping for a good takeover – a bit of authority, damn it! – and a 'return to God' to hold on to the whip with an iron hand! They've only got themselves to blame, these suicides who suicided their own children. Once they've been destroyed, institutions don't get back up any more than rites of initiation do: rendered derisory, they remain just that. And it's among these ruins that their descendants have to live. Under attack, they will no doubt say that they didn't realize; like their parents, the ones who went through the war, they'll confess to having 'obeyed orders': 'We didn't know.'

Oh yes, *we knew*! One day it will have to be held accountable, this spoiled, rotten, rotting, spoiling generation of ours. Yes, it's all very well, I admit, to try and retie the thread broken by my fault, my most grievous fault, by launching into this mission impossible. But I've got better things to do than to portray the ups and downs of the children of last century: things like altering the arrow of progress, understanding the work of the sciences afresh, salvaging the law, regaining politics, giving a new meaning to the word institution, deciding what our children should inherit. Having children again. Giving another meaning to the long history of the West, doing away with modernization. No, I haven't taken leave of my senses, I haven't become 'reactionary' with age, but I have gradually realized that we never have been modern. So I've asked myself if the signposts that used to mark the border between the religious and the irreligious hadn't shifted, if there hadn't, as a result, been a bit more room for a resumption of religious speech.

Who can tell today, for sure, what should go and what should remain? Who has the touchstone that distinguishes the 'reactionary' from the 'progressive'? No one does anymore. That's why I dare address by turns, like Janus, trembling on an ambiguous threshold, two disparate groups, the people inside and the people outside. Have I failed in my bid not to shock either group?

You can only see a horrible return to the past, an absurd dream of the restoration of Catholicism, an aborted attempt at modernizing Christianity, an impious secularization? Wait, wait, I've barely got started. Please, don't deduct from my account translation arrears that I'm not responsible for. Everything is against me, I'm well aware, everything points to my guilt, but only charge me for my transgressions, not for those of others – especially not those of my generation.

One thing's for sure: if we're going to start talking straight about these things again, without picking and choosing, without purifying (while picking and choosing, while making distinctions), we must not deprive ourselves for a second of reason and its tools. It would serve no purpose whatever to take each other's hands and dance, to the sound of the guitar, while waiting for a warm and friendly ambience to inspire us with sweet thoughts and brotherly smiles. In these matters of religion, there's no room for sentimentality. Attentive, inventive work on concepts and closely argued reasoning alone can make us more talkative. How can we hope to talk right if we start by humiliating reason, giving it borders in advance and then, when it stops at border patrol, offering to hand it over to another vehicle which we might call, say, 'faith'. I'm not familiar with such breaks of load; as they say on the railways, I don't trust this monstrous form of 'intermodal platform'. Either we're dealing with information content, and reason in its scholarly form carries on without limits; or we're carrying *containers*, and causing individuals to emerge, and there, too, we need all our reason, all our intelligence, all the subtlety of our reasoning – and there, too, there is no limit. The things I'm talking about are not irrational but require all our reason, the sole and only reason we have to survive with. We don't need any other light, any sudden revelation, any voice of conscience, any bolt of lightning from out of the vault of the heavens. If revelation there is, it will come from below, in the very thing that our intellect seeks to explain, to replay, and not from above, shedding false light on it.

Besides, what we call 'reason' in the ridiculous debate said to be 'between faith and reason' is nothing like the work of scientific reference, the setting up of those dizzying flyovers that allow us to grasp the universe, through streams of thundering transformations. Only double-click communication could have dreamed up constructing a scene where we'd have to choose between the rationality of Science with a capital S, and the irrationality of Religion with a capital R. What is called 'reason' in this comedy is more like a pile of nice, hard stones built up over the course of time which Punch uses to stone the naive, bombard the fortress of 'faith', bring down its walls and free the believers within from 'the hold of obscurantism', in which they are imprisoned by the 'dictatorship of the clergy'. There can be no use of 'reason' in this polemical sense, without a matching belief in the 'belief' of the faithful, who have built the indestructible citadel of irrationality using the stones their opponents threw at them! As a result rationality and irrationality increase, the besiegers becoming ever more sure of 'reason' while the besieged ensure, at each catapulting rock, that their only salvation lies in the 'irrational', beyond all reason. Besides, if they came to doubt the 'limits of reason', the limited reasoning of their rationalist opponents would fully justify them!

But it's a very long time now since the walls of Jericho came down, without drums or trumpets: this funfair 'reason' does just as little justice to the sciences as 'faith' does to religion. Transparent, immediate communication bears no more relationship to the work of information than access to the beyond resembles the delicate savoir-vivre of religious utterance. If there's one battle never to be waged again, this is indeed the one. In any case, we don't have several brains, no sixth sense, no other cognitive capacities than the ones we sometimes apply to vehicles that allow access to the remote, and sometimes to those that produce closeness. The means of transport are different, it's true, just as the paths they take are, and the wakes they leave – but not the driver and his passengers, who can't help but be the same. No, I have not lost my reason, I just want it to apply all its usual powers of reasoning to tracing the meandering path of these foreign words that seem to lift up those to whom they are spoken. As for the path of the sciences, I've applied myself long enough to that not to have to revert to it for the moment.

We do understand, though, the horror felt by fair-minded souls when they approach these issues. As soon as you abandon the reassuring path of communication and talk once more of religion, you do indeed seem to have to plunge into a form of *lie*, into the secret of an invention that, truth to tell, must *necessarily* lie. This experience does not surpass reason or everyday savoir-faire, but we do have to recognize that it isn't easy to take in our stride, because its very object consists in *routing* speech habits, in *preventing* the transfer of information, in *weaning us off* all communication. The thing that explains, without justifying it, the mistrust of the reasoners is that to tell the truth religion must in fact lie or, at least, if that word shocks, proceed to scholarly, no, to pious, no, to reasonable *elaborations*.

Yet this ongoing creation is something we accept without any trouble on the part of lovers, who never cease repeating the same love story in different words. When the woman implores her friend to reiterate his faith, she doesn't ask him to mime what he's already said before, or to say how he *has loved* her, in the compound past tense, but how he loves her now, in the present tense of the indicative. Without which the act of speech would remain ineffective; the lovers would take the name of their G. in vain. But between the two moments of time, before and now, a lot of things have changed: every cell in their bodies has been renewed; they no longer have the same concerns, the same relationships; other familiar expressions spring to their lips. A slow subterranean crawl has moved the goalposts. Consequently, one of two things happens: either the lover remains faithful to what he said before and repeats it word for word, but then he's telling a lie since he can't quite talk right, now, of their love; or, faithful to the demand of that love which requires him to address himself to the present, the lover says *something else* completely different from what he said before since the goalposts have changed: he has told *yet another lie*, this time in comparison with the tradition he wanted to preserve. Either he is faithful to that tradition, but then he lies since the words, when wrenched from their present tense, are only addressed now to a distant past; or he is faithful to the present, but then he lies once more since the salutary words *differ* from what has been said till then.

There is no way out of this paradox, except to change the subject and aspire to pursuit of the distant – except to stop the passage of time, or suspend the course of the sun. If you want to talk about love, about those words with their strange properties of bringing close together, it's always in the present, now, that you have to talk, and then, obviously, since the present differs from the past, the new talk, to be heard once more, must *differ* from the talk of the past. In other words, there is no salutary talk that can act and that *you have already heard*. Either it acts, it salvages, it redresses, what it's about is understood, and it's the first time it grabs you; or you've already heard it a hundred times, you know very well what it means, and that is certainly not what it's about. Either you manage to define love, and it is there, proved by this very talk, or you're talking about something else, but certainly not your love. (The woman is only too familiar with her lover's exasperating capacity for fleeing her injunction: 'You're trying to change the subject', 'Why are you talking about something else?', 'You're pretending you don't know what I mean', 'You don't have to justify yourself' – her companion will do anything, anything, to escape taking up the thread of their love again by laughable, frail little words that escape all accounting.) If we didn't have to settle centuries of arrears, nothing would be clearer than this particular demand; we would find it childishly simple. All lovers well know, as surely as the venerable fathers who turned the argument into 'the indisputable proof

71

of the existence of God': either we are talking about G. and he exists, since, as the philosophers say, his essence implies his existence; or we are thinking about something that doesn't exist, but then we are thinking about something else altogether, certainly not G. Always this dependence on the well-adapted word, this theurgy.

At first glance, this demand to speak always for the first time, to speak of the present, of you, me, here, now, seems crazy since it's hard to see how you can salvage the old words while remaining faithful to them. Either you chuck out the stale bits, but then you no longer have a single word provided by the tradition; or you piously preserve them, but then you are no longer faithful to the bringing close together. But it is indeed within this delicate machinery of the lie and the elaboration that the means must be found of finally paying those arrears accrued, of acquitting those dizzying debts that prevent us from salvaging our assets. The machine must be made to tick over again. Now, you can see that the choice is never just whether to keep on repeating like a parrot or to invent everything every time from scratch, *ab ovo*. And still less to modernize, adapt, localize. It's more a matter of understanding anew, based on present experience, what the tradition might well be able to say, lending us as it then does the words, the same words, but said differently. We don't have to innovate, but to *represent* the same. The *repetition of harping on the same old thing* is opposed by the *repetition of renewal*: the first seems faithful but isn't, the second seems unfaithful, yet it alone preserves the treasure that the other squanders while believing it's preserving it.

Lovers, for instance, don't judge the form of their

words according to their degree of oldness or newness. There's nothing more repetitive than the music of lovers; they always annotate the same story – theirs – but according to two modes, two tonalities that the crisis radically differentiates. Their story resembles two contradictory concatenations that become enmeshed like the arcades of a long street where, after a storm, puddles turn their quivering, shifting image upside down. Sometimes, they re-read the whole of their past as if it were merely the story of an ever-growing incomprehension tumbling down from the past to the present and thereby bringing indisputable proof that the future must part them forever. Sometimes, twisting, hedging, shifting, redressing, reinterpreting the same episodes, the same gestures, the same words, they weave a different, completely opposed story, threaded through the first, which proves, starting from now, through equally indisputable proofs, that they've always loved one another as they did the first day, better than the first day, and that the only future they have is to grow old together, ever closer. And each story exists inside the other one in the manner of a remorse, a risk, a heady presence – so much so that we can never take for granted what the present instant proves. Like those fun images in which the form and content are reversed according to the way you're accustomed to looking at them or the angle at which you approach them, these two narratives coexist so comfortably that the same present instant can become either the end of an affair that is finishing today, or the starting point of an affair that is resuming afresh. All the episodes are the same, none is similar. *Hic est saltus*, this is where you have to jump.

73

Why have we remained so skilled at the gymnastics involved in the lovers' crisis when we have become so rigid whenever we try to use it as a template for understanding the religious experience afresh? Is it because of the lack of resemblance between the private history of couples and sacred history? Yet the only difference between them might well be the scale of the group, the ambition of redemption, the choice of the people to be saved. Let's have another go at capturing the big by the small, the sacred by the profane, the unacceptable by the familiar. It's as if the same tradition could appear in either of two states: solid or gaseous.

A word received that is addressed to another time and to another place immediately loses its initial freshness, its efficacy; by construction, it appears to us now as no more than an artificial obstacle to understanding what it's about. There is nothing to be done. By opening our minds, we can indeed believe that it had the power to transform for good those it was addressed to *once upon a time*, but we don't really give a hoot about that anymore. Such is the solid state of the tradition, its mortal weight. Yes, but the thing is: as soon as I finally understand, for myself, what it's about, I also begin to understand what it was that so deeply moved those people, too. The same way that lovers, when they emerge from their crisis, reinterpret their life together, here we, in turn, are again gripped by the same retroactive movement of time that flows from the present and heads for the past, illuminating opaque writings by the bright light of day: 'Everything has become clear, I was reading them without understanding.' Yet, every one of those now intelligible expressions remains foreign, exotic, none resemble those we employ, they are all untruthful through the sole fact that each is addressed to a place, to a moment in time, to a different person from history. Yes, but in every one of those places, in every one of those moments, on every one of those individuals they had the same effect, which I finally understand for the first time the same way the contemporaries of the Pentecost were affected by it: 'So, that's what they were trying to say? How come I didn't get it earlier?' As this dazzling sequence spreads, all the moments of redress in a way link up, one by one, adding another story to the story of different places and times – no, it's the same one, the story of being brought face to face with the same revelation and the same redress. As far back as the revelation of this sameness goes, so goes the feeling of forming a people with those you then discover, with amazement, to have been addressed, despite the distance that separates them from us, as we are, in the same terms – which nonetheless don't formally resemble each other in the slightest, since the definition of the 'same' has also changed. The tradition has changed state, it has gone from solid to gaseous, light, we could even say spiritual if the meaning of the word had itself been renewed.

It gets horribly complicated. But having got to this critical point, we must not falter no matter what. We must not go back on our word. We must not be afraid to split hairs if, at the end of the day, we manage to get back to simplicity. No effusiveness, no sentimentality. No point thinking that a direct return to infantile piety would make us more faithful. We can't talk either correctly or directly about the words that redress. Sadly, to understand this subtle (but simple, oh-so-simple) machinery, we'd need all the savoir-faire of the engineer, the meticulousness of the scientist, the acuity of the witness, the scruples of the aesthete – not tó mention the lightness of the angel.

Let's take it slowly, step by step, and look seriously at the machinery of the truthful lie, that modus operandi by which *well-formed* religious expressions are produced within the tradition of the Word. An idiom used to seem clear to a certain people thrown into a situation that has become foreign in our eyes. This same idiom, repeated as is by another people in another situation, no longer has any effect, since time has passed. Through the simple flow of minutes, what was transparent is now obscure. The word has gone from being a conduit to being an obstacle, the lying truth. Its simple rehashing could only add another layer to the growing wall that divides interpretations from each other. Yet, those ancient peoples obviously had to try to draw on words and rituals from within their tradition, from within the treasure amassed by their predecessors, even if those forms of life couldn't correspond any more closely to what they wanted to say than their own words would later be able to satisfy their successors. To mark the transfer from one time period to another, the words have had to be made to undergo minor but violent *twisting*. This twisting is not adaptation, deformation, adjustment, modernization, but total transformation, since, instead of referring to the distant past, it forces us to refer to the present. But how can we see to it that an utterance taken from another time, another place, another people, becomes conducive to this kind of radical transformation? By grasping it in such a way that it becomes *inappropriate* for all other uses. By coming up with a series of inventions, translations and tricky manoeuvres that stop us from being dragged back to the past, to a distant world, whenever we hear it and forget what it's all about as we stand around stargazing. We are not necessarily going to swap the venerable utterance for a newly minted one – for nothing proves that a recent expression will be better adapted to the job – but, by obliging the old one to refer to the present, we are going to put a stamp on it that will renew it for a brief moment. That is the secret of elaboration: the tradition finds itself effectively revived, twisted askew to get it to bring forth the present once more. We've paid the cost of transportation by a radical transformation that hasn't modified what we have moved.

There's nothing mysterious about the general form of this exegesis, it is even discouragingly mundane. What could be more tedious than the expression 'I love you'? Untold millions of people have used the same formula. *Soooo boring.* What about 'I'? That empty pronoun has served as a mask for all the beings on this earth – those at least whose language uses the first person singular. What could be more impersonal than the personal pronoun 'you', which designates all the 'you's without distinction? And what can you say about those expressions, which the linguists call deictics – 'me', 'here', 'now' – by which we refer to what is most present, most immediate, most concrete, by means of the most hollow, the most universal, the most abstract? We can see that the words themselves, the old refrain of personal pronouns, won't be enough for the lovers to express themselves each in their own language and say what they have on their minds. But they only have at their disposal the words their tribe has bequeathed them. No matter how creative they may be, they are not about to reinvent the grammar. On the other hand, they can't remain mute. In the end, they have to speak to each other again: 'Why don't you say something? Why are you keeping quiet?' So, to break the ice again, they're going to add to the never-ending refrain, to the nauseating needless repetition, by a sign, a shock, a shake-up, some small thing, some hint of something that comes from within and puts its stamp of authenticity on the mundane phrase. The interlocutor will receive the two messages at the same time, as in stereophonic sound, the one involved in the repetition of rehashing and the one involved in the repetition of renewal. He is going to be able to use the one as the key to unlocking the other: either he decides to cancel out the love talk when he detects the banality ringing out in the background (*soooo boring*), or he is deeply moved by the old refrain behind which he hears an appeal for reconciliation. Just as the battery icon on a portable computer indicates by flashing that the batteries are in the process of recharging as soon as you plug the computer into an electric current, a dazzling tension is added to the worn-out words, signalling that they, too, at that very moment, are in the process of making sense again.

So, we don't judge the truth of words of love or religion by their degree of oldness or newness, but by their way of linking up so as to conduct, or not conduct, the energy that will estrange or reconcile, kill off or save. It doesn't much matter whether they seem dated, patinated, venerable or, on the contrary, new, spruce, flashy. They make no sense on their own, in any case: it is only the chain, the procession, the link-up that makes any sense. Actually there are two senses, according to whether the links of the chain are connected by that which has conveyed them intact, or by that which has totally transformed them. It's as if each link had two active sites, two channels, two forms of connection: one signalling the indefinite distance between the diverse situations scattered over space and time, the other marking, for each situation, its resumption, its recharging, its twisting that has made the preceding phrase intelligible, for a time. But alas, by definition, the small innovation, the small trembling, the hesitation, the concealment, the resumption, the withdrawal, the lie, the elaboration, that allowed a people to appropriate the language of their predecessors, becomes confused for its descendants with that which creates an obstacle to *their* understanding of the message. The innovations of a couple of lovers aimed at telling each other their love in the worn-out words of romance are no use at all to another couple who have to revive two worn-out expressions, not just one: the new one lost its freshness as soon as it was said, since it was addressed to perfect strangers and so can't be of any use to us, here, now.

In other words, thanks to the first mode of connection, the phrases are easily conveyed through archiving and repetition, but they *get blocked* every time they are moved in space and time: to unblock them, you have to start everything again every time from scratch, but with no other recourse than the poor words you've received as inheritance, squeezed dry, pounded, distorted and twisted. So, two stories coexist, interwoven like the two stories of the lovers: the first one runs through the series of expressions that have been false, then renewed, then falsified once more – so much so that these sedimentary layers of half-lies and half-truths end up creating the impression of a vast shambles we must at all costs escape from if we don't want to suffocate. And yet the second one, humble and secret, retroactive and subtle, flexible and stubborn, links together two moments of revival in the course of which you see that, through the diversity of successive expressions and successive disappointments, it has always been a matter of saying the same thing again to diverse peoples, who are deeply moved in the same way. The unbearable lie becomes the dazzling truth: 'Oh, so that's what they *were trying* to say!' Considered according to the *longitudinal* series of repetitions going from the past to the present via rehashings and deformations, history is a web of lies, religion a prime example of non-sense; grasped again according to the somewhat *transversal* series, revivals going back from the present to the past, history becomes truthful again, and religion (at least in this tradition of the word about the Word) a prime example of the advent of sense.

It's impossible, though, to stabilize once and for all the relationship between these two visions, these two stories – any more than the lovers, once reconciled, can believe they'll be united and close forever. Religious speech is like the fabric Dante talks about in *Paradise*, which keeps shrinking: for it to keep its length, bits have to be added to it endlessly. Lies and elaborations are constitutive components of religious expression, since utterances and rituals must always be brought forwards or backwards if they're to continue to be true in the present, and we can't perform such sliding, such snaking movements or drifts, except by twisting venerable words round, wrenching them from their past context to get them to say something topical that they have never signified. Such inventions, embroidery, additions, are essential to reviving the message, but scarcely are they articulated before they interfere with the understanding of the descendants who must seize this old twisted speech *and the old addition*, in order to decide either to understand better thanks to the intense work of renewal done by the preceding generation, or to understand *less well* due to the accumulation of falsities, which has become truly dizzying over the course of time. Anyone who thinks they can do better and put it more simply so as to make religion at last directly responsive, without interference or intermediary, will always do worse and put it more obscurely.

There's nothing particularly extraordinary, anyway, about such crossovers of meanings. We all experience the difference between the longitudinal series and the transversal series whenever we become attentive to the rhythm emanating from a piece of music that is nonetheless continuous. There is the flow of time, which always moves forward, with a beginning, a middle and an end, and then there is the beat, which always returns, marking the same cadences and the same tones and engendering the transversal figure of the cadence, based on the lateral flow. We can never separate the two: without the continuity of the melody, we would never hear the rhythm. And yet, the rhythm is indeed written

in obliquely, as though between the lines, through repetition, askew as it is, within the continuity of the time
flow that carries the listener away. It is not external to it,
superimposed, but internal, created, *beaten out* by the
passage of time.

Inspired phrases and texts have the same structure:
they tell a story that has a beginning, a middle and an
end, but at the same time, they beat out a cadence, they
create a rhythm, by endlessly reviving the same movements. They shatter temporal continuity to stop us from
becoming attached to their longitudinal series, from
letting ourselves get carried away by the meaning of the
story, which is most often anecdotal, until we become
capable of hearing, until we become attentive, until we
manage to listen to the transversal, vertical series, that
message that is threaded obliquely inside the other. But
this message, like the rhythm of percussion instruments,
is not external to the story: it is internal to it. It is *that*
story, revived, interrupted, given rhythm and cadence,
repeated. They can't be separated any more than the
form of a jet of water can be separated from the flow
of drops that embody it by renewing it every second.
We can certainly say that such texts 'save' since, in their
movement, they imitate what they talk about: in the
course of the continuous narrative that passes, stands a
time that doesn't pass. What they say, these sacred texts,
these rare texts, is that you don't defeat death by throwing yourself outside time, but by beating it out in a way
so as to give it rhythm, give it cadence and structure. If,
say these texts, they were to fail to express such a reversal in the flow of time, then death would in fact, in the
end, win. In the modern era, through the invention of a

82

repetitive style, Péguy recaptured this pulse I'm stuttering away trying to theorize anew.

In the light of this machinery, which has nothing irrational about it even if its moving parts are rarely the object of any description, I understand better why it would have been impossible for me to *purify* religious discourse: impurity is part and parcel of the blueprint. Depriving ourselves of lies and embellishments meant retreating into the ineffable or into the banality of a sentimentality as universal as it was insipid. There is no path to take other than the difficult one of twisting, of losing meaning, of archiving, rehashing, reviving the revival – and so on and so forth, down through the years. There is no religious speech that isn't hesitant, stuttering, embarrassed. Unless we stop the meaning mill and, out of laziness or cowardice, let the arrears of translation accrue. Then we would speak straight and clear, but to listeners who wouldn't understand a thing. In religion, you don't find any directly addressed speech – any more than, in the sciences, you find clear utterances that aren't heavily rigged. Let's spurn the naked but chilling truth, and always opt for the truth warmly dressed in its veils of padded velvet.

I also understand better what was so pathetic about the 'mental reservations' solution. I don't have to translate untruthful words into an idiom that's finally appropriate and accurate, for no extra layer of language, no matter how current or how new, is preferable to the most ancient, the most hackneyed, the most mawkish, if its recharged version lacks spark or dazzle. And the other way round: once the twisting, the revival, has been done, all the different versions stack up, one on top of the other (but this is not an addition, more a multiplication) in an alternative recapitulation that justifies the pious lies of a humble shepherdess every bit as much as the sublime inventions of a learned mystic. What I claimed to transpose into my internal language is exactly word for word – no, that's just it, no word is the same – as what was said in the inept language – no, that's just it, it is straight and right – that I wanted to translate. Translation doesn't progress in the least, doesn't innovate in the least, except by allowing us to understand today that the ancients already understood exactly the same thing, which it's therefore completely pointless to repeat in other words. Yet, if we were to conclude from the temporary sameness of these two forms of contemplation that it was now superfluous to revive anew the work of translation, then this truthfulness is forever lost, just as the love between the lovers is lost as soon as they stop repeating it to each other, for it's not a matter of conveying a treasure intact through time, but of filling the coffers by once more risking the lot – the whole kit and caboodle! – on the gaming table.

But then, if I no longer have to purify the message or add to my mental reservations, I'll finally be able – without my conscience being torn apart, without agonizing – to recite my *Apostles' Creed*. I'll be able to speak right and freely; my tongue won't get stuck to the roof of my mouth anymore; I won't have anything to blush about anymore. By redeeming in a single stroke the mortgages that weighed so heavily on my shoulders and those of my descendants, I'm going to be able to talk without torment, I'm going to be able to rejoice in earnest. Alas, the day still seems pretty far off when we'll be able to take possession of our inheritance, since a new phenomenon of interference comes and slows everything down, in the manner of an unjust taxman suddenly demanding exorbitant duties. This is because another form of narrative crops up and creeps in between the longitudinal series of narratives and the transversal series of revivals. The engine has barely ticked over again when it once again chokes. A mob of creditors come rushing in, the debt once again grows vast.

As it happens, the devil, kept at a distance for a moment, finds in the forking essential to any revival of meaning a dream opportunity to get us to fork our tongues. Great is the temptation, when we find ourselves in the grip of a chain of traditional utterances (that thereby include the ancestral forms, plus their revival, plus their exhaustion, plus their new revival), to *simplify* a switch that calls for so much skill, so much attention, so much contemplation, so many scruples. It happens surreptitiously, as if, while you're groping about in the dark, you were suddenly offered the support of a helpful handrail. This, as we know full well, is the support provided by utterances bearing information. As in a shunting operation, the branch line deviates so imperceptibly that you don't realize you've swiftly changed rails and that rather than face real difficulties – the revival, now, of a demanding message – you are about to get lost in a maze of thornier and thornier questions that you can never see an end to. To get us to chase rainbows, the devil sends us one of his countless damned souls: the demon of *rationalization.* He whispers its temptation in our ear when we're at our most fragile, when the finest discernment is required, at the very moment when we hesitate to chuck out the old form for a new one, without really knowing whether we're dealing with a moult or a mutation.

'Faith' has been pitted so relentlessly against 'reason' that it seems hard to claim that religion can be *rationalized* to the core today. And yet, the thing that prevents us from coming to grips with it again is not the foreignness of its words, or the archaic nature of the impulses behind it, but the prodigious mass of rationalizations that has made it, with the passage of time, only more incomprehensible the more people have tried to shed light on it. 'Rationalized' does not mean 'reasonable' or 'rational', but only that, every time a new translation was necessary, people tried to substitute an information issue, as convenient as it was incongruous, so as to spare themselves the tension of revival. In giving the impression of talking more logically, they slipped from a mystery of cleverness to a mystery of absurdity. This paradox – no, this diabolical trap – is something we have to outsmart.

The story of Noah's Ark is a typical example of an elaboration that must have allowed a people remote from us in time to revive an earlier message we no longer have direct access to. Travelling through the narrow straits of longitudinal history, the meaning has been lost. Unless we situate this venerable tale within a comparative mythology of the ancient world . . . but then we would be drifting towards archaeology, we would no longer be seeking to transform anyone whatever through a tale that no longer says anything to anybody. Travelling through the narrow straits of transversal history – at least, I persist in thinking so – there must be some sort of access, sealed off for the moment, that might enable us to retrieve what was able to move that people deeply to the point where they expressed its revival in such a striking invention, taken from a myth available at the time, unless it transfigured some fabulously ancient geological event. What would correspond for us now to what they were trying to represent by the flood? Punishment? Renewal? Dependence? Hope? Recreation? We still don't know. But let's now assume that, at the very moment when we're hesitating, we are seized by the pruritus of rationalization to the point where we ask ourselves: 'How big, in fact, was Noah's Ark to be able to house all the pairs of animals comfortably? What was the wood it was made of? How much hay did Noah and his sons have to stock up on? How did they avoid the rapid spread of epidemics in such a confined space?' By posing such questions, we become aware that something doesn't ring true, that there is a kind of dissonance, a discord, that we've committed an error of reasoning – but what is it?

Have we tried putting questions that are too reasonable for a manifestly unreasonable tale – which would make no more sense than asking a lunatic who thinks he's Napoleon if his wife's name is Josephine? Are we trying to apply our poor human reason to revealed tales whose mysterious ways will always be hidden from us? Are we forcing ourselves to take literally a picturesque story that's trying, naturally, to say something else? No, these three solutions, the first too critical, the second too pious, the third too metaphorical, would actually prevent us from hearing how far our questions are from being in the right key. Our mistake comes from somewhere else: we have quite simply tried to establish, between ourselves and this tale, a bridge of reference that would allow us to transfer information from the past up to the present, whereas the text was hoping to convey the transformation of its readers *from the present* – their present at the time – back to the past. We've committed a category mistake, the same as the mistake the lover makes when he answers 'I told you last year' to the woman who asked him if he still loved her.

If rationalization is so demonic, it is because it makes the detection of these category mistakes so impossible. It thereby makes us commit second-degree faults, reflexive faults – the most serious, for they bear on the very conditions of utterance. It transforms the tale into a matter of what's reasonable or unreasonable, whereas it's about something else entirely: expressing the difference between words that accede to the distant and words that produce proximity. If we need to attack such rationalization, this is not at all because it involves reason in domains where it has no business being, but more because it claims to reserve the use of reason for conveying information alone. It thereby prevents reason from getting down to work providing us with the skill to talk about what might, now, in relation to the pathetic story of Noah and his dove, convert us. It suggests to us that we have *reasoned badly* whereas we have, quite simply, *behaved badly*.

If rationalization can tangle us up like this, seemingly at whim, this is because it remains at the same time, of course, powerless to reason in earnest with the usual tools of computation, instrumentalization and modelling – in short, of formatting, the formatting of information. Like belief, it mimics the moves of reference, but without paying the price for doing so to the last. If I seriously get down to measuring Noah's Ark so as to house all the species in it – from the elephant to the cheese-mite, from the baobab tree to the buttercup – I will arrive at a dimension such that all the humans of the day together could not have made even one rib of it. What do I do, once I've reached that point? Continue along the path of veridiction? But then the whole of the story becomes so absurd that it will evaporate like the morning dew. Dig in? Carry out excavations on Mount Ararat, as American creationists are doing, hoping to find some vestige of Noah's Ark buried in the ground? But even if we were to uncover some, what inference could we possibly draw from it? Nothing more than the existence, on top of a mountain, of a piece of wood that we could date with carbon 14. So? Why should I care? I'm not asking you whether you loved me, all those years ago, but if you love me now. I'm not asking you to take me by some perilous, controversial path to a remote place and a bygone era in order to give me a fragile and temporary mastery of them, but to lift me right now out of this deadly estrangement the crisis has plunged us into. Just as incapable of pursuing scholarly, serious and disputed access to fossilized vestiges as of stirring the whited remains of our present love, rationalization will leave us high and dry, dumbfounded like Buridan's donkey, without being able to bring us either knowledge or conversion.

The worst thing would be to yield to temptation and *answer* the demand for rationalization. We yield to it all the more gladly as we think we're doing the right thing, to the extent that it allows us to put a bit of order into this mess of stories received by the tradition. By making the tales a bit more logical, a bit more reasonable, but without being able to see either the work of information or the movement of conversion through to the end, we will, at the end of the day, make them even more opaque, thereby adding new confusions to the hotchpotch of old peculiarities. The true scandals – in the sense of opportunities for understanding – now find themselves, as you rationalize them, drowned in a sea of improbabilities that only increase the scandals – in the sense, this time, of obstacles to understanding, opportunities for stumbling.

We will say, for instance, that 'Jesus is risen'. If already we can no longer understand those words, it is very tempting to ask ourselves the common sense, yes common sense, question: 'So then, the tomb must have been empty?' Before we know it we're adding an episode to a story that has accordingly become both more reasonable – since a *connecting passage* has been added – and more unreasonable – since the initial lack of understanding over the sense of the word 'risen' is now capped by a second lack of understanding over the empty tomb episode. And since we then find ourselves saddled with a double lack of understanding, the demon of rationalization whispers to us that the way to get out of this is by a third eminently commensical suggestion, a reflex reaction any good housekeeper would have: 'The proof is that the shroud is lying on the floor of the tomb.' Other stories will follow, other embroideries, other inventions, pious lies, but lies all the same, in which the blood-stained cloth will be stage-managed a thousand different ways. Then, like children who start telling fibs and then try to get out of it by inventing more and more improbable ones, we force ourselves to 'prove' the preceding inventions by other inventions. Until, suddenly, in mid-course, faced with the scepticism provoked by all these whoppers in reasoners whose inclinations we've played to, we change our tune once more and admit that we're dealing here with mysteries too deep for human understanding. With admirable liberality, wherever we no longer understand the mechanism for producing meaning, we indulge in handing out miracles. Then, still hesitating, annoyed at having embroidered so much, and stricken with remorse at having strewn miracles around so rashly, in a new twist we start sending relics off to the laboratory, taking DNA samples, slipping electrodes into the skulls of clairvoyants – bits of scientific procedures that we then give up on as suddenly as the rest as soon as we decide that they've led us *too far* down the paths of information. When the demon of logic interferes, the particular regime of religious speech becomes indecipherable, and rationalization, the true madwoman in the attic, leaves behind her everywhere a trail of chaos, as incapable of doing the serious work of the sciences as of getting on with the job of religion. The devil has triumphed: we will never be able to talk about these things again.

Thanks to rationalization, inspired texts have been made *apocryphal*. Instead of the cracks in the narrative gathering meaning, they've been covered up or encrypted: they distract, they whip up, they mislead. The Apocrypha anaesthetize like opium. We no longer hear in them the transversal history that alone allows us to grasp what these venerable writings were talking about. The reader's attention flies off to ancient times: death will triumph, since the direction of time has once more been reversed. Because of the varnish of logic that has been laid over these little stories, we're able to let ourselves sail down the long calm river of causality that moves us from the past to the future, instead of going back upstream from the present to the beginning, through constant, ever renewed, effort. Instead of carrying out at great cost the tremendous task of repeating the message so that it's comprehensible to those it's addressed to, we content ourselves with *deducing* the consequences based on the premises, getting the reader to take part in a spectacle that he watches from the outside and that no longer has the aim of transforming him: in any case, everything was there, in embryonic form, from the beginning, the passage of time only made concrete its ineluctable *necessity*. (The lover is very familiar with this abyss of iniquity into which he has often plunged, with great pleasure, pretending not to hear the woman's generous injunction, and casting about everywhere for some pretext that will let him deflect her appeals, just to avoid having to take up the meandering journey of his love again – in the manner of a salmon abandoning itself lazily to the current, instead of swimming back upstream, in a series of leaps that defy all gravity, and regaining the spawning ground where he was born.)

You say the expression 'Virgin Mother' has been incomprehensible for a long time? Who cares, for thanks to a stream of piled-up rationalizations, we now claim that 'Mary born without sin' existed 'for

all eternity' and did not know 'the original sin of
Eve's children': a 'divine plan' hidden from the eyes
of mankind had from the beginning always foreseen
Adam's sin and kept in reserve the woman known as
the 'Immaculate' – a connecting passage added rather
late in the day to put an end to violent battles between
rationalizations for people who already could no longer
quite comprehend how a 'God' could have been 'born'
of a simple woman. The whole Holy Story will find itself
replayed as the unfolding of reasoning, editing, a *logical*
compromise. Of course, the edifice is fragile, it rests on
a dizzying number of hypotheses all made absurd by the
passage of time, and yet, it's not its irrationality that
makes it untruthful but its *excess* rationalizations: all
these pious inventions replace the equally dizzying leap
from the present event with the simple deployment of
a deduction. They soon start talking about the 'coming
of the Lord', as we would speak of the Big Bang and
the mutation of particles it involves 'as a consequence'.
In order to leap from one present to another present,
we've saved ourselves the hard labour of translation,
confining ourselves to the mechanical game of linking
causes and effects. We've even gone so far as disfiguring
Providence, turning it into a simple prospect, a paltry
forecast. Rationalization manages to turn religious
utterance on its head. Everything has become merely
logical – without managing of course even so, despite
all the tricks of apologetics, to convince a single decent,
reasonable thinking person. If, parallel to this, we've
maintained without transforming it the notion of an
all-powerful, all-knowing 'God', who is outside history,
absolutely stable and enduring, standard and yardstick

93

of values and assets, then there is nothing more to be done, the meaning of these texts is gone forever. From now on, it is in vain that time passes, in vain that the present occurs, in vain that the texts are read. Nobody is charged with grasping them again, gathering them again, anymore; there is no more theurgy; the people composed of neighbours has been disbanded; there is, then, strictly speaking, no more religion. Yes, death has won. Only the devil is smiling about this, into his goatee.

But then, the solution is pretty much ready-made: just as restorers of paintings remove the additions, varnishes, revisions and second thoughts of successive restorations which obscure the canvas in order to give it back the dazzling hues of the past, so we have only to get rid of all these rationalizations to recover the original sense. If the delightful tales of Jesus' childhood sound like late additions, compiled by the anonymous authors of the Gospel known as 'according to St Luke' to make the hard-to-swallow business of the virgin birth less illogical to Greek ears, then take them out! If, scrubbing a bit further, this miraculous birth appears to be the result of a rationalization made necessary by the previous invention of a now hard-to-grasp expression, 'Son of God', well then, drop that dogma. If, cleaning still more intensively, we discover that that expression, in turn, makes no sense to a Jewish ear, that it's probably an a posteriori rationalization of another formula, spoken by the historical Jesus: 'The kingdom of God is nigh', then scrape off that troublesome formula too. If the tale of the empty tomb appears to be an embroidery added later to smooth out a pretty rocky tale of resurrection, cast it aside – and, while you're at it, chuck out the relics, the shroud and all those plaster virgins with breasts full of milk and eyelashes full of tears, along with all those wooden crucifixes oozing blood that clutter up the sanctuaries. Come on! Let them give us the meaning at last, disencumbered of all these rationalizations which, in striving to make it clearer, more reasonable, more ductile, more logical, have only heaped up the false problems, multiplied the artefacts, without quite taking the paths of reference through to their conclusion, even so. Since most religious mythologies do not derive from irrational inventions but, on the contrary, from incongruous rationalizations that interfere with the conversion effect by deflecting it from its aims, let's get back to the only narratives capable of saving those who read them.

Alas, this solution is as unworkable as the purification solution. If we begin to go down the road of 'derationalization', of 'demythologization', there'll be nothing left. Besides, the example of paintings should give us pause for thought (even if it may cause the sometimes heavy hand of curators to tremble), for in removing the additions, the second thoughts, the varnishes, the successive restorations, we risk obtaining only a pale surface, as far from the original canvas as the dark impasto we claimed to be renovating. At each restoration of meaning, religion, instead of coming closer to us, recedes in time: all we have left in front of us are a few snatches of Aramaean phrases spoken by a certain 'Joshua', a native perhaps of Nazareth, overloaded with footnotes and inaudible across a long history of inventions and interpolations that has become forever opaque. The cure is worse than the disease. To avoid a rationalization that embroiders, we've fallen into a derationalization that eliminates. To avoid a varnish that yellows, we've removed the pigments that gave the painting its density. Vacuum cleaning. Mister Clean. All gone. (Some people reckon that, if we seriously had to clean Leonardo's *Last Supper*, which was already restored once in da Vinci's lifetime, not a stroke of paint would remain and tourists would have to be satisfied with stunned contemplation of a completely blank wall!)

This is because derationalization may well do a thorough job of cleaning, but it always stems from the same pious referential intention, and, instead of allowing us to grasp once more which vehicle lets us convey across different ages narratives that can convert every time, leaves us hanging in limbo: neither in the past, nor in the present, neither in the authentic, nor in artifice. We are entirely deprived of the means of knowing how to repeat the message across a history whose essential properties are the lie, the invention, the embroidery, the exaggeration, the edit – in a word, elaboration – but without actually being offered the principle that enables us to distinguish the salutary innovation from the logical raving, even so. What's the good of cleaning the message's façade if we don't understand the movement that must, of necessity, mess it up? It's not the cleanness of the result that matters to us, but the original impulse, the modus operandi, the labour, the matrix that allows us to keep on producing new messages. No one can commit to no longer deforming or reforming the religious message, since deformation and reformation *are part* of the message, the only means of making it heard. It is the principle behind this deformation, this reformation, this elaboration, and it alone, that we have somehow to grasp if we are to speak freely of these things.

To avoid misunderstandings, people thought the right thing to do was to rationalize: result, misunderstandings mushroomed. But the solvent of derationalization is far too caustic. To extricate myself, I don't need *readymade* narratives, I need to be let in on the secret of the machine that produced them, and that could generate them today *de novo*. My mind has been cluttered up with this whole business of the authentic and the inauthentic, the original and the copy, the age-old and the tacky, as if we all had to take ourselves for little Viollet-le-Ducs charged with restoring Notre-Dame de Paris by rebuilding, in the middle of the nineteenth century, a cathedral that would at last be truly gothic. But there is no more call to modernize religion than there is to give it back its primitive purity, because there is no more of a modern world than there are primitive worlds. Religion goes all archaic or becomes contemporary again according to whether you distance yourself from, or come closer to, the source, which always produces new narratives strictly identical (completely foreign) to the old ones. The original is not in the past but in the present, always in the present, the only asset we have.

A less drastic solution is suggested to me. These narratives only sound strange to our ears because they have 'another meaning', a 'hidden meaning', a 'symbolic meaning', one that never dates. These tales, they say, mean *something else* that doesn't involve them either in the rational or in the irrational. So it's pointless to vacuum clean them. The suggestion, this time, is no longer to derationalize with a whole lot of solvents, but rather to propose a definitive translation that is at last reasonable.

Great, fabulous, but in that case, give me this something else, this truth that's supposedly concealed beneath naive appearances. I do indeed suspect that expressions like 'Noah's Ark', 'Jesus is risen', 'Son of God', 'virgin birth', 'empty tomb' are not there for their own sake, that they take the place of something else *that is not there*. But if so, then lead me, please, to what they refer to, don't just entertain me, annoy me, outrage me with expressions and images that are no longer truthful. You don't know where that might be, you say? No, no, no! Don't tell me they're inaccessible, too, that we're dealing with mysteries too remote, for it's me we're dealing with, now, here; if you want to transport me once again into the distant, then no thanks, I much prefer slow and steady vehicles that amble along, sure of the reference. At least I know that with them I can go anywhere without ever running into roadblocks beyond which it's forbidden to think. You're not going to pull that old stunt again of deflecting me even further towards the distant when it's the near, the origin, the present my soul longs for.

Ah? We can go there? Great, so show me the plans and maps you're holding in your hands; give me the decoder that lets us view clearly what was encrypted in these messages, till now indecipherable. What? You want to transform 'Son of God' into 'expression of the divine'? Then I still prefer the first expression. If you have the audacity to propose 'oedipal mother' in place of 'Virgin Mary, Mother of God', I still prefer to belong to this Church here than to that sect there. If you detect 'Indo-European myths' whenever they talk to me about a 'trinity', without my understanding the first thing about it; if you hear 'eternal wisdom' when I read, without grasping it, the 'Sermon on the Mount'; if by 'Jesus' you understand 'the highest moral authority of humanity', then I think I'm going to abandon your symbolic meanings and content myself with the letter, which seems to me to be more precise, more deeply moving than this insipid 'spirit' which, according to you, it expresses only clumsily.

Why is symbolic reading so seductive? Because it allows us to tuck the letter and the spirit conveniently away, side by side, like two coffins laid in a vault. All the difficulty of hearing religious messages stems from the fact that they're forced to refer to the present state of those they address, by replaying utterances with a violence, a twist that makes them inappropriate for current information consumption or communication. Which is a difficulty that their being written down in a book, forever detached from the felicity conditions of utterance, of course only increases – especially when the 'divinely inspired' Scriptures are judged immutable and holy. It's because of this gap, this *inappropriateness*, that religious utterances give such a strong impression of strangeness that they seem clumsy, patchy, deficient, unresolved. Their authors went to great pains so that when listeners hear them, they can't feel committed by an information logic that might transport them far away into the distant, but are gripped instead by a logic of transformation (yes, it is indeed a logic, and even a mechanics, as lovers know only too well) that sets them straight again and makes them close.

But if, thinking you're doing the right thing, you start to *smooth out* these tales further to make them more coherent, easier to swallow, less bristling with contradictions, less bizarre, then instead of making them more comprehensible, you'll be making sure they're even more ill-adapted to the injunction they bear within. Interlocutors are really going to think that, when they hear 'expression of the divine', it's about capturing a piece of information whose accuracy and authenticity have then only to be verified – whereas the expression 'Son of God' at least had the advantage of sticking in our craws, so we either had to vomit it up or finally understand what it was about, which has nothing to do with 'divinity'. The clumsy, literal expressions of the tradition are rough enough, bristling with enough bumps, riddled with enough cracks, covered in enough parasites, gnawed at by enough improbabilities for the revival of the message to be able to hang on to them and twist them back in the right direction. But the symbolic expressions that people are trying to substitute for them, slick, logical, audible and shaped like suppositories as they are, can do nothing other than slide effortlessly through the networks that further remove them from their proper use. By becoming even more inappropriate to the religious regime of speech, all they do is awkwardly mimic the utterances of information without actually enjoying their capacity to convey. By yielding to symbolism, we have lost on both fronts, yet again. The more you make religion modern and acceptable, soft and digestible, the less you are faithful to its specific order of difficulty. It is against symbolism that it should be said: the spirit kills, the letter alone gives life.

So let's admit that religious expressions do indeed mean *something other* than what they say, that they, too, do indeed designate a spirit not to be found directly in the letter, but that this spirit has nothing to do with another meaning hidden by the first. It is what does in fact circulate, literally, in another *sense*, in another direction, transversally *despite* the continuity of the tale. Yes, they are *legends*, but not as in tales of wonder, more as in those cartouches you find at the bottom of maps offering guidelines on how to read them. The thing that makes the symbolic solution so insipid is that it accumulates the hidden meanings by tucking them away one behind the other, like parallel layers, without actually altering the *position* of those layers. Well, it is this change of position and it alone that matters to us in retrieving the movement, the gradual swing from the longitudinal series to the transversal series of narratives. With the symbolic solution, the second layer of meaning finds itself *behind* the literal expression, but it occupies exactly the same position as the first. And the solution doesn't get any better if you imagine, in a sort of gnosis, a third meaning hidden behind the other two, but always parallel. The religious movement we are hoping to seize again is not like a second screen behind a first screen, like a face behind a veil, like a mystery behind its manifestations, like a message behind a rebus, or hieroglyphics. These stacks of successive layers, all these veils piled on top of one other like so many petticoats, keep our eyes turned in the same direction: they confirm us in our desire to accede to the distant, to the ever

101

more concealed. But it's not a matter of turning our eyes towards the distant; it's not a matter, either, of seeing through untruthful appearances to seize the hidden truth, but of bringing our gaze back to the near, yes, to our neighbours, to the present, which is always waiting to be recaptured.

The spirit is not to be found *behind* the letter, beyond it, but *in front and on this side of it*, in the manner of the cadence beaten out indirectly thanks to the continuous flow of the melody. The thing that makes religious expressions so hard to understand is not a hidden meaning to be found above some Jacob's ladder whose successive rungs are lost in the clouds and that only the rare privileged few manage to scale. What makes the meaning elusive is that it's so simple, so visible, so close that it lies prone before us, abandoned by all: a child could pick it up – a child did pick it up. Yes, those dated words meaning something else, but, no, that something is not remote from us. Only its proximity makes it hard to understand. As long as it remains remote, we know with absolute certainty that it's not what it's all about. The relationship is not that of a model to its prototype, of a façade to its interior, of a phrase to what that phrase *is trying to say*, but the skewed, twisted, quirky, warped, polluted relationship of an utterance to *the person trying to say it*. That in a nutshell is the eminently simple difficulty.

But you don't really want us to stay with the letter even so, surely? For us to become literalists, fundamentalists, like those who remain persuaded that you can open the Bible like a railway timetable or a geology treatise, that the sense of each phrase will leap out at us, directly, without any interpretation, as clearly as if I say in prose: 'Enter Hamlet'? No, of course you don't, since that literal solution would boil down to abandoning religious sentiment for good by no longer imagining any other speech regime than the one involved in double-click communication. The creationists and other literalists can no longer even remember that there was a time when people spoke to designate something other than access to the distant. Instead of showing their irrationality and their archaism, they reveal on the contrary, in their obsession with reference, how far they are both rationalized and modernized, since there no longer exists any way for them to judge the truth of an utterance except by its capacity to tell the truth *in the manner* of a transfer of knowledge without the slightest mediation. They no longer make any distinction between the assertion of a holy text – 'The Bible claims the world was created in six days' – and the oracle of a talking clock – 'At the third stroke it will be 8.30 a.m. precisely' – except that the first seems to them to be more reliable and more admissible than the second … How could you get the biblical texts more wrong than by confusing them with writings informing us about the state of the world? How could you scorn the messenger angels more than by transforming them into optical fibres only good for faithfully refracting light? How could you say the name of 'God' more falsely than by judging what he says in terms of kilobytes?

Yes! You can do still worse, all you have to do is completely abandon the referential angle and start *aestheticizing* religion. From that moment you can forget about making these texts, these pieces of music, these rituals say anything other than what they express, but without actually giving them back the spirit that brought them to life: let's stick to the letter, let's transform all these risky elaborations into more or less brilliant *œuvres*. That's it for the quarrel over symbolic, literal or spiritual readings. 'Yes, it's true, you're right, religion doesn't mean a thing anymore now. But it will bring you so much beauty, so many treasures, so many thrills, so many tears, so many palpitations! Ah, the motets, the baroque angels, the tympanums, the gold chasubles, the solemn processions, the children's choirs ringing out under the Roman vaults in clouds of incense . . .' Salvation through art. The genius of Christianity. An apparently charitable solution that comes down to killing it off once and for all.

There is indeed, it's true, some resemblance between religious and artistic regimes of utterance: as opposed to communication, such utterances have a common front, since they are both accused of not faithfully informing; both share the same need to embroider, to lie in order to tell the truth; both depend for being understood on the participation of speakers deeply moved by œuvres as much as by angels. We can see why these resemblances are enough to make them quiver in concert; that religious speech has never got going without dragging in its wake all the beauties it could muster; that art has never shone without the gods smiling. Yet, nothing allows us to confuse them. Art doesn't save or resurrect, except through metaphor. It can transform, but not convert. This is because the direction of its élan is exactly opposed to that of religious speech. If it can't be confused with the laborious paths of information either, this is indeed because, in spite of everything, it still turns our over-accustomed gaze towards the remote, towards the distant, towards the foreign – even though, contrary to the travail of reference, it never worries about exercising control over the places it allows us to reach. It is because of this *accessless access* to the far away that it can enthral, fascinate, amaze. But that's just it, art is too mysterious, too spiritual, too haunted by the beyond, too enigmatic, too innovative, too perverse as well to accompany religion for long in its meanderings. It disturbs, it invents, it lures, it does not create the people formed by those who understand the tradition that we were reading till then without understanding. To entrust art with the fate of those holy words would make no more sense than entrusting them to the vehicles of information. Religion must disappoint the aesthete every bit as much as the scientist.

Could it be that, from this moment on, by abandoning the false succour of rationalization, of the symbolic explanation, of artistic satisfaction, I am finally getting closer to the true sense of these phrases made hackneyed by such long usage – or rather that they are getting closer to me? Could it be that the thing that would make these tales, these rituals, these gestures truthful won't be found either *in themselves* in their literal expression, or *behind* them in the themes they are allegories of, or *in their wake* in the unfolding of their logical consequences, but will finally reveal itself through their rough bits, their deformations, their stitches, their dissimilarities, through all that makes them inappropriate for normal information consumption, unfit for any literal reading, dangerous for any form of aesthetic digestion, incomprehensible for any 'communicator'? That, on top of their explicit message, these tales include an encoding, an encryption, that won't emerge as another message behind the first, but will take the form of an injunction thrown down before the message *implicating* the person to whom it is addressed? Not an implicit sense behind the explicit sense, but an *implicating* sense before the *complicating* sense? Could I finally be getting to the end? Could I finally be capable of speaking clearly once more?

The friars of the Dominican Convent of San Marco, in Florence, commissioned Fra Angelico to do the fresco there representing the episode of the empty tomb. I know enough art history to see that such a painting 'illustrates' the evangelical tale and to spot the codes of the programme, typical of the era as well as of this form of piety. I've read enough critical interpretation to know that this episode is only a late elaboration, that it belongs to those rationalizations that obscure the message in trying to clarify it. The infelicity conditions have covered this admirable fresco so well that the sense is lost for me as a simple tourist passing through the narrow cell today. All that's left to me is to enjoy some aesthetic pleasure and the pleasure, less acute, by which I verify that my knowledge of history 'applies' to this particular case. Yet, little by little, as I stand there in contemplation, the image begins to crackle, causing ever more visual peculiarities to leap to the fore: the holy women arrive at the tomb, but it's empty and they see nothing; an angel sits, indicating the hollow tomb with one hand and, with the other, pointing to the apparition of Christ risen bearing the palm leaf of the martyr and the standard of salvation – but the women can't see this apparition, since they have their backs turned to it. 'He's not here' says the angel in the text. Where is he then? What's going on in this utterly familiar illustration of a theme that's been revisited over and over again?

A monk, in prayer, drawn with half his body cut off by the frame as if he shared the floor of the cell with me and had been projected onto the fresco, looks without seeing, his eyes downcast, at the whole scene. The painter must have put him there so that his figure will help me make the transition by implicating me in this curious story in which no protagonist sees anything *directly*: neither the women, nor the angel, nor even the monk – nor me as a result. Yet I'm the only one to see, behind everyone else, the painted apparition of Christ. But that's just it, it's only painted – a fine and delicate film of pigments. What do I see? It's not here either that what we have to seize again happens. The angel's finger points to it for me: 'He is not here, he is not in this dead fresco, in this cell as cold as a tomb.' I was a bit lost: there was nothing to see. I am saved: I understand the meaning of the episode. 'He was dead, he is risen': it's not back down there in the past that the meaning must be sought, but now, for me, here.

What does this fresco *represent*? That transitive verb has numerous direct objects: the empty tomb scene; Dominican piety; the talent of Fra Angelico or his disciples; the work of conservation and enhancement done by Historical Monuments of Italy. But what else does it represent? A message encoded in the previous message and which says: 'Look, this is how it should be read. Take care. It's not about representation at all. That's not where you need to look. He is not here. See where they've put him.' The legendary sense, the sense of invention, has indeed been added to by a legend, in the sense of instructions for use. Within the theme, lodged inside it, something comes along and shatters it, complicates it, transforms it, transfigures it, makes it unlike itself, inappropriate for any habitual use, any aesthetic, erudite, informed, historical consumption. Through a series of minuscule inventions, tiny shifts, little visual nudges, paint smears, the fresco reinterprets the text which is in turn made up of other inventions, other elaborations, other discrepancies, improbabilities, interpolations, oddities that make them both – the text that revives other tales and the fresco that illustrates it – capable of signifying something else entirely from what they explicitly say. The longitudinal layer of representation is gradually replaced, as my meditation broadens, by a transversal series that also *represents*. But what? What did it represent? Yes, that's exactly, literally, it: it re-presented, but this time we're dealing with an intransitive verb with no direct object: it *presents again*, and hey presto, the story is transformed although it seemed to me at first, when I stepped into the cell, forever remote in time and space. If the object of the fresco is not here, in the tomb, and if he is no longer far away in the past, that's because he is present, here again, before my eyes. At last, I can see clearly, and what I see is no longer empty, but full.

If the lovers had to paint their unprofferable G., they too would resort to these legends, these instructions for use, these second-degree expressions to designate, within their discourse, how we need to hear them to properly hear ourselves. They too would multiply the dissonances and the discrepancies, the dissimilarities and the twists, to make felt properly the fact that they're not talking about ordinary, accessible, manageable things, but that, look out! they're starting to talk about love, about dangerous, difficult, complicated things that have the strange particularity of making them exist, at that very moment, of implicating them, of making them become people capable of talking to one another freely – and their tongues loosen as they get closer, progressing, in a few hours or a few minutes, from the most embarrassed expressions to the sharpest repartee. They too would at first multiply the negative expressions: 'That's not what it's about, and you know it; you always try to run away, to turn away; you do everything you can not to understand; listen to me, just listen to what I'm telling you; look at me!' They too would add interfering, transversal, tangential elements to the usual forms, so as to redirect the other's gaze, to force their attention, to force themselves to be in close contact again. A tremor in the voice, tears, an angry gesture, maybe a kiss, any little thing that comes and deflects, crackles the usual tone. The moment the crisis is temporarily resolved, they too would feel close and present. And yet, in this whole business, which is a matter of their life and their death, not one atom of information will be conveyed. They won't be any the smarter, wiser, or more artful for it – except that, by acquiring the experience of the crisis and its resolution, the next ordeal might find them less helpless, a bit faster on their feet.

But then, if it's true that even a story as worn-out, elaborated as late in the day as the one about the empty

109

tomb, revived centuries later by a Florentine painter, can, for a wretched tourist, five hundred years after that, once more represent what it's all about, this means that the weight of rationalizations is not as fatal as it appears. Smack bang in the middle of the figuration of the legendary theme –'Look, yet another fresco *about* the empty tomb', 'Look, yet another *illustration* of the Annunciation' – another legend appears, not against the light, but as though spread along a series of incisions, of cracks, of dissimilarities; a legend about what the theme means once more in the eyes of an informed and regular visitor who is changed, for a brief instant, into a convert suddenly recalled to presence. Behind the infelicity conditions of the rationalization that deduces the present from the past by applying the general theme (empty tomb) to a particular case (Fra Angelico in San Marco), we can distinguish, as though woven through the image, inserted tangentially thanks to small visual improbabilities, the felicity conditions that once more become as fresh as on the first day – not exactly fresh since centuries have gone by and we will thereby be able to go back, from the present to the beginning, and *realize* at last what the ancient tale was trying to say for a very much greater number of the faithful scattered over much longer time spans: 'He is not here, why are you looking for the dead among the living? Why are you throwing yourself by these words into access to the distant, when it's a matter of the near and the present?' Grasped in the primary sense of 'representation', the painting is transparent, offered to our aesthetic or scholarly enjoyment exclusively; grasped in the second sense of 'representation', it becomes opaque again, demanding conversion. It no longer means something remote; it means that someone came close.

So, is it possible to elude the ingenious trap with which the demon of rationalization tried so hard to trip us up? In itself the invention of a new form doesn't have to be dangerous as long as it inserts enough *warnings* about the right way to take it. The very moment I understand the pictorial conventions used by Fra Angelico to make the worn-out episode of the empty tomb gripping again, I also understand what energy, what faith, what theurgy was able to see to it that a true discipline should add, somewhere in the course of the first century, the tale of the empty tomb which he embroidered on to the older corpus of the Passion, in order to comment on it faithfully, yes faithfully, through a striking, pious invention. The *faithful invention*: that's it, I'm getting closer at last to the source, the modus operandi of all the narratives.

When I entered the cell a frightening distance separated the author of the anecdote, Fra Angelico, and me, but now the abyss has shrunk before the sole and unique presence, represented three times, capable of giving rise through these three different mediums – the narrative, the fresco, my pathetic essay – to three inventions, which are offered up to the discernment of the faithful. Those who elaborated the episode of the empty tomb were embroidering, of course, but *they weren't lying*, at least not as long as they encoded in their initial elaboration instructions for use that allowed it to be properly grasped and properly understood. It is we, and we alone, we latecomers, who *retrospectively* turn our ancestors into simple liars (pious liars but liars nevertheless) if we forget to grasp their invention and

111

fail to hand down and add, in our turn, the right legend, the right way of reading properly that they put in their tales for us to protect them in advance, as though by a talisman, from any wrong reading, any regular reading. In other words, every elaboration conveys at once the poison of the chain of logic and the counterpoison of its revival. It is on us, now, today, that the fate of this treasure depends. According to whether we take it as a simple deduction of consequences – a historical tale that goes from the past to the present – or we go back from the present to the past, stressing the bumps in the text – a religious tale that has never sought anything other than to convert the distant into the near.

Let's look more closely at, say, the Gospel known as 'according to St Mark'. Let's not try to aestheti-cize, rationalize, purify, demythologize this round-up of awkwardly pegged-together pericopes. Instead of taking these scattered pearls for bundles of information that needs to be reconstituted within a homogeneous spatio-temporal framework in keeping with the recent habits of historical narrative, let's do the opposite and try hard to keep the gaps, the unfinished bits, the breaks, the implausible details. Above all, no filling in. Let's not add anything to or remove anything from the innumerable stitches, sutures, cicatrices, link scenes, interpolations, bumps. Let's accept for a time that no information is given to us about anything at all. Or rather, at the same time as the longitudinal tale strings events together in a chain, from the preaching of John the Baptist right up to the Ascension, drawing our gaze towards the distance, towards Palestine, towards the Roman Empire, let's become attentive once more to the instructions for use repeated in the text so that we learn to take it the right way, to read it the right way, to understand it the right way. Immediately, this narrative, considered the most rudimentary of the four, becomes extraordinarily, miraculously clever. Understood according to the longitudinal series, it tells a wondrous story; listened to according to the vertical series, it tells us *how* we have to understand any story of salvation – so that we can produce new ones. The two movements, the continuous one of the narration and the discontinuous one of the repetition, like the warp thread and the weft thread, weave a single scarf, verse after verse. It's like a double-entry table where the lines record the obvious meanings, one after the other, and where the columns, struck by turns like the keys of an organ being played, slowly fill, revealing to the amazed eyes of the reader a second vertical meaning inscribed tangentially within the longitudinal flow.

First column: *tags* that no effort at plausibility bothers to smooth out ('In the wilderness, John . . .'; 'And when even was come . . .'; 'And he saith unto them . . .'). Second column: *ruptures*. Lives abruptly change course ('Follow me. And he arose and followed him'); sick bodies are healed; drastic demands are made ('And if thy hand offend thee, cut it off' [9:43]; 'We have left all, and have followed thee' [10:28]). Third column: violent *reactions* to these sudden ruptures; people are constantly 'struck with astonishment', 'sore amazed'; they become anxious, they ask themselves 'what manner of man is this' [4:41], 'by what authority doest thou these things? and who gave thee this authority to do these things?' [11:28] Fourth column: *incomprehensions*, blunders,

113

exclusions. People never stop mistaking what is happening ('Is not this the carpenter, the son of Mary?' [6:3], 'That is Elias' [6:15], 'Art thou the king of the Jews?' [15:2]). All the participants are on the wrong foot, 'Having eyes, see ye not and having ears, hear ye not?' [8:18], no one gets it, no one understands: a rich young man wants to follow the rabbi, but he very quickly loses heart; the apostles quarrel, have their doubts, make mistakes, ask who is the greatest among them; always getting the wrong end of the stick, they lament the lack of money ('From whence can a man satisfy these men with bread here in the wilderness?' [8:4]), sleep when they should be watching, betray when they should be faithful; they're all wrong, right down to the multitude who, between Barabbas and Jesus, choose Barabbas; right down to the putting to death, the ultimate lack of understanding about the event under way.

Obviously it's not easy to understand what's going on here. Hence the following column: the *cautions* and refocusings column: 'Why reason ye, because ye have no bread? perceive ye not, neither understand? have ye your heart yet hardened?' [8:17]; 'Be not affrighted' [16:6]; 'Watch and pray' [13:33]; 'There cometh one mightier than I after me' [1:7]. Every error of interpretation is the object of an abrupt reminder that obliges you to refocus attention elsewhere ('Get thee behind me, Satan: for thou savourest not the things that be of God, but the things that be of men' [8:33]). Do you bother observing the sabbath, or not? That is not the issue. You want a sign? No sign will be given to you. You are scheming between marriage and divorce? A man and his wife are one flesh. You think the Son of man can't die?

114

He will die. Will they finally understand? Yes, and that's the sixth column, which isn't as full as the others: the column of *recognitions* and satisfactions. Some people manage to recognize at last what it's about: first of all the author ('The gospel of Jesus Christ' [1:1]), the Father ('Thou art my beloved son' [1:11]), the demons ('And unclean spirits, when they saw him, fell down before him, and cried, saying, Thou art the Son of God' [3:11]). The heavens open, bodies are transfigured, you wake up among the dead. But as soon as recognition occurs, silence is imposed; that is the function of the seventh column. 'And he straitly charged them that they should not make him known' [3:12], 'neither said they any thing to any man; for they were afraid' [16:8]. Eighth and final column: the *envoys*. It's not a matter of just bringing the continuous, horizontal thread of the tale to a close, but also of ending the transversal, discontinuous rhythm of the other story: 'And he ordained twelve, that they should be with him, and that he might send them forth to preach' [3:14]; 'But go your way, tell his disciples and Peter that he goeth before you into Galilee: there shall ye see him, as he said unto you' [16:7].

What is this text saying? In its continuous reading a heap of anecdotes, objects of belief, of glosses and wonderment; in its discontinuous, transversal reading, not much, not much at all, really. The disappointment is fundamental, essential: we are shocked, surprised; we don't understand; we are warned to pay attention once more; for a few brief moments, we grasp what it's all about at last, suddenly satisfied; then we immediately lose the thread; we start looking elsewhere, only to repeat the whole business over again. And it starts

115

again, the same refrain written tangentially into the endless repetition of the same story of salvation. What, you still don't get it? Yet, stuck right at the centre of the text so that no one can make any mistake, tales of parables explain reflectively, explicitly, knowingly, how the text is supposed to work, how it is supposed to be taken. The parable of the sower provides the instructions for use: if your heart isn't properly prepared enough, all these seeds sown will wither in vain.

What, you still don't get it? But the last line, the fringe on this scarf, on this table, ought to illuminate us for all time, for an instant: doesn't this tale of resurrection say, clearly, that it's a question of life and death, of presence and absence, of today and not of days gone by? It's not just the end of the longitudinal story, it's also the *lesson* of the transversal story, the repetition, the retelling, the reflective interpretation of the whole affair. The tale of the resurrection is not endowed with information, as if the text ended in that apotheosis; it is endowed rather with a warning: this is how you should read the rest of the story as a whole and especially, how you should repeat it, starting from now, in the future. It's not a question of death but of life. Yes, this Gospel, once it is redressed, does indeed become *inspired* since it has made itself unusable for any reading to do with information, communication, entertainment, aesthetics, wonder; since it has destroyed from within any referential temptation; since it has covered itself in safety devices so that we don't go looking elsewhere, in the past, for what appears now with dazzling clarity, waiting right here, in front of us.

It's a frightening responsibility: either we respond to

the temptation of logic and add a new layer of rationalization to these sedimentary strata whose weight crushes us, or we finally take our turn reviving the rhythm of the whole set of legends by reviving what they have always tried hard to get us to say properly and to represent properly. If it's true that we can't clean up the rationalizations, if it's true that no effort at purification can bring us any closer to something authentic, it's equally true that each of these successive elaborations does not actually constitute bad material even so. Besides, we don't have a choice. There is no way of speaking, no matter how erudite, cleaned-up, derationalized, tarted up, disinfected or disciplined it might be, that could take a single step in the right direction, since it is precisely in its cracks, weaknesses, opacities, dissonances that is revealed the injunction it has always tried hard, through crazily intelligent inventions, to make heard anew. There is no right way to speak religiously. Who would dare claim that he has the right, the precise, the definitive, the orthodox metalanguage to talk about these things? You might as well decree that, from now on, the lovers should only speak of love to each other in French! There is no religious speech that is direct. There are only *infra*languages, those spoken by the generations that came before us and which we need to make truthful in turn, just as they made those of their predecessors truthful by twisting them thoroughly through a series of elaborations the devil alone can make us take for simple lies. But does this mean there are no more arrears? That the debt is wiped out, the mortgages lifted? That the difference between the truth and the lie is as fine and as radical as the difference the lovers experience between proximity and distance? Everything is false in religion, we have to reject everything; everything is true, down to the last comma, and we must not change one iota. It depends on us, on you, on me alone.

So, there exists a form of original utterance that speaks of the present, of definitive presence, of completion, of the fulfilment of time, and which, because it speaks of it *in the present*, must always be brought forward to compensate for the inevitable backsliding of the instant towards the past; a form of speech whose sole characteristic is to constitute those it is addressed to as being close and saved; a kind of vehicle that differs absolutely from those we've evolved elsewhere to accede to the distant in order to control information about the world.

This form of utterance is difficult in itself but only to the extent that it must always be revived to begin its work of designating, purifying, resurrecting and redressing its interlocutors again.

It finds a sort of prefiguring, a scale model of its felicity conditions in the language of love.

Even though it is in no way irrational, it always appears untruthful in the eyes of those seeking either to convey information without distortion – the adherents of double-click communication – or to preserve intact the meaning of these utterances without reviving them, in another form, for another time, for other people.

As such distortions are inevitable, there is no way of understanding one's own moves other than by in turn slipping into this choreography – easy one moment, uneasy the next – of revival, wear and tear, retranslation, loss of meaning . . . and so on and so forth. This dance will serve as a test to sort the clever from the clumsy. Woe to anyone tripped up by an obstacle! This rigorous selection process doesn't mean we're dealing with things sublime, forbidden or commonplace, but that this incredibly simple movement of revival must be either accomplished, or uncomprehended.

To maintain some chance of dancing on the right foot, successive generations seem always to have taken great care to accompany their discourses, their rituals, their images, with a second level of instructions for use inserted tangentially into the first-level anecdotes, injunctions that constantly remind us of the right way to understand them, the right way to speak truthfully. But with the passage of time, these injunctions, these ways of speaking, will always be misunderstood, and that is why they have to be revived always, through new cautions.

Once they are revived, all ways of speaking, the new and the old, the humble and the most elaborate, become equally truthful again as though they had only ever designated the same thing. Those who hear them ringing out clearly again, having become close and present once more, will form a same people confirmed in its vocation or a freshly designated people, one that will never coincide, by definition, with any linguistic, ethnic or cultural borders whatever. Yet, the very minute they lose the sense of these utterances, the assembled locutors will be dispersed, as foreign to one another as the sons of Babel. As soon as they retrieve the sense of these utterances, they will form a people who will increase every time in time and in space.

The moments of revival and faithfulness and the

moments of dispersal and unfaithfulness weave two forever entwined stories whose final fate remains, to this day, undecidable. Or rather, the decision lies now in the hands of whoever grasps the present text.

This speech regime has to do – but how? – with what is known, in shorthand, as religion, or, at least, with one of its traditions, the one elaborated little by little around endlessly revived commentary on the Word and the Spirit.

Ah, but then, the word has finally been restored to me! I'll get back the love of words I lost. I'm free again, without shame and without fear, since, instead of ready-made utterances, I now own a machine for manufacturing them. Won't I, in turn, at last be able to produce entirely new ones? Instead of *negatively* defining, as I have done till now, the felicity conditions of this extremely perilous regime of utterance, won't I be qualified to produce salutary words *positively*? Sadly, things aren't that simple, for I'm still terrified of proffering the name of the unpronounceable G. Of course, I no longer have to wonder how it's possible to translate tales of salvation for them to be both faithful and new. But the task that awaits me is much more fearsome: I now need to understand *what class of beings change according to how they are addressed*. I have nicely reconstructed the stratum of transformations that convey these deeply moving utterances through time and space, I have nicely eluded the referential trap, avoided the false problems created by double-click communication, but I still don't know what a form of speech that evokes beings who appear and disappear depending entirely on *how they are said* might be trying to say. How can the existence of real and helpful beings depend to such an extent on saying, on simple *ways of speaking*? What class of existents is this? In wanting to revive them, haven't I irremediably destroyed the force of these discourses? If so, that's when I would have said the name of G. in vain.

This regime of utterance, we now realize, is not complicated: it is simply *fragile*. The smallest thing, the slightest puff of air, the tiniest time lag, and suddenly it means nothing anymore. Which is only natural, since it seeks to save definitively – temporarily – the person it addresses through words that do what they say. When people started, round about the sixteenth century, to develop powerful means of conveying information without distorting it, it's not all that surprising that the religious vehicle seemed, by contrast, so slow and shaky that it could only be cast aside so people could go faster and farther. In the face of the power of metrology, what indeed could that ancient way of establishing – backwards, retrospectively – universals of such variable geometry do? Things only got worse when, to safeguard its hold, religion tried to emulate the spread of emerging empires by claiming, too, to speak with authority of the distant, to control the flows of information, and to dominate at a distance thanks to strict control of standards and canons. Its role was then limited to managing a domain that has since shrunk like a shagreen. Thinking it was saving itself, it lost its way irretrievably, incapable as it was of moving on imaginatively by transforming itself as it had till then always done. With every new century, it has had to dump ballast to stay afloat. You only have to look at how the churches, at least in western countries, have gradually emptied. When they realized the nave was too vast, they fell back on the chapel, abandoning to the tourists holy places handed over to national heritage protection organizations; then the chapel felt too big: they took refuge in the crypt; when they started to feel all at sea in the crypt, a handful of them squeezed into the sacristy. And in the near future? They'll hide in a cupboard and won't dare come out again. Congregations float in naves that are too big for them like dwarves trying to wear the richly coloured chasubles of giants. And outside, there's nothing for people to put on, they go completely naked. Religion confined to a mere parson's nose.

Maybe, at the time, the Zeitgeist – this is a hypothesis – didn't know how to innovate by investing simultaneously in two such different forms of propagation, and that, to develop the scientific and imperial machine, the venerable machinery of religious speech needed to be set aside for a while. Are we any better placed today? Now that the sciences have enough history and patina not to dazzle us anymore, are we capable of mastering their subtle advances without necessarily having to scorn the movement specific to bringing people close together? If I still dare speak, it's only because I think I can brush aside the shadow that the ways of science once cast over the ways of being produced by religion.

To start with, over the particularity of this kind of speech of being thoroughly *reflexive*, of persisting in saying, time and again, how we must say what is to be understood, without ever telling us, once and for all, what that is. From the point of view of the sciences, this is an insurmountable weakness; from the point of view of religion, an essential property. Have the length and breadth and depth of this particular disappointment been measured? Everything speaks of the word but this word says nothing. It doesn't say the nothing, it doesn't speak of the void, it doesn't address nothingness – which would still be a way, if completely negative, of turning us towards the distant, of referring. No, it's tirelessly content to talk about the way to speak *properly*, and to represent the right way of representing properly. It talks about the word, it verbalizes the word. Even when you think you're sending it up, you still express it aptly: 'It preaches the *good* word.'

To translate the Greek word 'gospel', people always talk about the good *news*, but no one yet has ever explained, in all these centuries, *what* this famous news *was*. In terms of conveying information, of kilobytes, of an erudite message, you have to acknowledge that this is a colossal loss of energy, an inconceivable waste, a truly cosmic con. Hundreds of thousands of pages have been written over thousands of years by millions of believers, in order never to say exactly *what* this news is, even though it moves them to the depths of their soul, and they're ready to surrender their goods and their life, since, they claim, with transports of joy, it has already saved them. But what are you waiting for, then? If it's a message, upload it! Religion – how many bits? Not a single one. Not even a single pair of nought and one. This is because it offers something better than information transfers: it transforms the absent into the present, the dead into the risen.

But that's impossible! You can't reduce all religious passions and reasons, that long series of transformations, elaborations and inventions, to this single derisory expression: 'ways of talking'. How dare you claim that every one of these words whose meaning is lost on us today – 'God', 'Word', 'Spirit', 'Risen', 'Church' – conceals pure ways of saying, simple reflexive injunctions, operating at a second level, on the manner of speaking properly, on the good word? You might as well try getting a pyramid to stand on its head. How on earth could the power of religion be expressed in such a convoluted form of discourse? As if you could start talking about these things by saying: 'In the beginning was the Word!' You're playing with words. You're adding an intellectual's trick to the long trickery of the clerics. And yet, that is indeed how the Gospel said to be 'according to John' starts, though he doesn't explain the content of the word, either, but only the way we should receive it. It is indeed with those feeble words – feeble in comparison to the powerful transports of information – that we really should familiarize ourselves. I have no other intermediary if I want to get back the habit of talking fearlessly about these particular things.

When the lovers are in the grip of their dizzying crisis, and find themselves indefinitely estranged from one another, they really can't count on the *substance* of their love anymore. They can wonder all they like: 'But, in the end, we've loved each other a lot and for a long time, haven't we? Our love will get us through this terrible impasse, it will overcome everything else', they sense perfectly well that this particular little 'God' can do nothing more for them, that no force of inertia will hold them together a single day more. But later on when, in the middle of the crisis, they discover the narrow door that suddenly propels them from distance to proximity and they sob in each other's arms, laughing at their past stupidity, they're delighted to see that their love has returned, strong and powerful, *at the same time* as the fluency of their speech. And at that moment, yes, they can count on the love they've been able to renew. When their love was a substance they hoped to draw on the way you draw a cheque on a current account, it could do nothing for them and they remained distant, mute, downcast, stubborn, waiting for it to pass: nothing was passing – happening – between the two of them any-more. When they look at each other again, talk to each other again and once again something *happens*, they find themselves in each other's presence, and then their love, beyond and between them, gets back its freshness and effectiveness, its force; it can once more support them forever, they are (relatively) absolutely sure of that.

If the lovers wanted to characterize the particular metaphysics of their love, they'd say it comes in two states: the first is *substantial*, but then it's powerless, it has no force of inertia; the second is *effective*, but then that's because they got back together again, they finally had a good talk, *talked properly*. Either their love is a substance whose attributes serve no purpose, or the lovers are capable of bringing out its attributes and then, yes, effectively, their love *stands underneath* – which is precisely what the word 'sub-stance' means – all the shows of tenderness and affection. Over this period of grace they've just entered, it would never occur to the lovers how much the newfound love that brings them to life again depends on fragile conditions of utterance

125

which they had such trouble discovering the secret of, however childish that secret may be. But if they grow away from each other again, then, yes, effectively, nothing about this love that has vanished into the clouds will pull them out of the hell they've let themselves fall into. Such a reversal of the respective role of attributes and substance seems horribly tricky, and yet we perform this gymnastics of mixed ontology every morning.

Is it still possible for us, today, to benefit from the lovers' intimate and fragile exercise in order to try and understand the expression 'ways of speaking', respecting *at once its dependence on the conditions of speech and its substantial reality*? This is how I've transformed my initial question: can we speak once more about these things? Is it possible, with the tiny flame of personal love, to rekindle the fires of religion? (And is it actually desirable, when we know what havoc those fires have wreaked, how many fanaticisms, stakes, autos-da-fé were ignited in their wake?)

I'm well aware that no form of collective life exists any longer, or any commonly accepted language game that would allow us to magnify sufficiently the experience of love so as to speak, not of the micro-people formed by lovers, who are always 'alone in the world', but of the great virtual nation drawn up by those who finally realize what their predecessors meant when they wrote and when they read the Scriptures. The way along which the faithful multitudes once passed has become as invisible as those country lanes so choked with brambles that you need to consult the records of the land registry to rediscover their traces. We need to hack out other paths, if possible in town. Are we still capable of that?

126

I've said too much, I've taken too many risks, I have to go the whole hog. Have I expressed myself properly? Have I been clear enough? I've probably committed all the sins, reinvented the wheel of all the successive heresies; no doubt I've shocked, hurt and offended those within as well as those without; I deserve to have a rope hung round my neck with a millstone at the other end and for me and it to be thrown in a lake. Yes, maybe, but at least I haven't added a single day to the translation arrears. Let those who can say as much throw the first stone.

To speak about the word, I have no solution other than to join up words separated by thousands of years and rub them together again to bring forth a spark of light. This is both hopeless – the distance is too great – and very easy: they speak of the same thing, of the present, of bringing close together, of representation. If, for instance, I dared speak about the 'working of the Holy Spirit' the way the lovers speak about their love, if I gave it the same substantial reality within the same dependence on speech, would we find that expression so enigmatic? Of course, if I say: 'The Spirit will renew the face of the earth', I start looking for a substance, a substantive with the attribute or property of the action of renewal. In so doing, I distance myself. I look upwards. I lose myself in the clouds. But if I say: 'The *renewing of the word* can, for a certain time and for a certain people, be called "spirit" and even "Holy Spirit"', don't I get just a little bit closer? Don't I manage, for a different people, ours, and for a different time, mine, to grasp again more precisely the movement at issue? There is nothing more in the substantive 'Spirit' than in the verb 'to renew'. In the first expression, I put the substance before the attribute, the essence before the existence, the name before the thing, the cart before the horse; whereas in the second, I begin with the utterance and I *end* with a substance: I start from existence, from its fragile dependence on the right word, and I *recapitulate* it after that in an essence. First I make the thing exist and only after that do I name it. Everyone will agree: if I manage to bring about the real presence of the thing, the exact name doesn't matter so much since, as on the day of Pentecost, we can come up with *plenty of others* according to the times, the peoples, the places. So, to assert that the 'Holy Spirit' is merely a 'way of speaking' is not necessarily to distance ourselves from its reality in order to turn it into a simple play on words; it is also to descend from the inoperative and remote substance in order finally to do again what the thing itself says: 'Thou renewest the face of the earth' [Psalm 104:30]. In the one case, I give a hint of a reference; in the other, I stutteringly look for a formula using the *present participle*: 'renewing'. Is it better for us to hear ourselves participating in the spoken thing in the present tense, or to keep intact the name of a substantive that can do nothing for us and can no longer even be heard?

But renewing what? What does the revival allow to be revived in turn? What is the penultimate link preceding it? Of which way of speaking does it allow us to speak properly? We know very well, we've got it, there can be no further doubt on the subject: we can't hope for any message conveying, no reference transfer, not one bit of information will be given to us, not a single sign. We will only grasp the reality at issue when

128

we possess, when we receive, the right way of uttering these words. This link between utterance and material truth is neither a paradox nor a mystery, but the felicity condition we have now recognized – which all lovers practise without making a meal of it. This 'renewing', which certain people call 'Spirit', has rejuvenated prior talk that would long have been incomprehensible to our ears without this revival. Which one? The revival of another present participle known in certain circles, at certain moments, as 'Jesus'. No doubt about it, without the spirit of renewal that expression no longer has any meaning for us, unless we change tack and go on a search for information, uncovering, in the company of archaeologists and historians, what might have come to pass, a very long time ago, in Galilee possibly and then in Jerusalem. But this conveyance towards the 'historic Jesus', which has its own usefulness, its particular grandeur, its specific demands, its rigour, its seriousness, can't be confused with the usefulness, the grandeur, the strictness, the rigour and seriousness of the conveyance that occupies us now – now, not yesterday. In both cases it's a matter of evidence, of reality, yes, of objectivity, but the first of these things is indefinitely distanced, masterable only by the paths of reference, whereas the second is within our reach, and it masters us by making us close and present. We still have to learn to let ourselves be held in its grip.

Having got this far, there'd be no point in breaking off our journey on the pretext that we might run up against some unfathomable mystery; no point either in imagining that we could make some rough and ready compromise and replace the mute expression by some other more reasonable, more plausible or more purified expression. I've explored each of those paths: I've found them all to be forever blocked off. It's also pointless throwing ourselves, in despair, into the bottomless pit of belief. We have no other way, truth, and life but the path, anchored in the present, that links ways of speaking, the good word and the good news together by making them clear and distinct once more, for each place, for each people, for each period in history. In itself, the expression 'Jesus' is meaningless: it designates the deployment of the whole translation chain, it is coextensive with all the operations of conversion, realization and meaning. Its substantial reality, its corporeality, only holds for as long as all these attributes find themselves manifest and linked. The manifestations come first and after that 'what' is manifested. Or rather the 'what' is merely the manner of retrospectively regrouping and holding together all the manifestations of the process of bringing close together again, the linking of all these successive movements, the infinitely extended thread without which all these pearls would be scattered. Without the movement of translation, there is no sense in the substantive 'Jesus'.

The fact that we're not dealing here with just another of the accessible and masterable things, but with another operation of renewal, is something the word tells us with accuracy and precision since this 'Jesus' is also called the 'Word'. What does it say in turn, this word that is begun again, uttered anew? Nothing that has anything to do with information. Nothing that directs our gaze towards access to the distant, nothing that allows us to climb up into the clouds, to reach another world. Once again it preaches the good word. Exactly as the spirit restated, differently, for other ears, what the word once said to his own people, he in turn restates what, for other ears, was lost: 'The time is fulfilled'; 'The kingdom of God is at hand' [Mark 1:15]. Two ways of speaking are slotted together, allowing us to hear with amazement a *third*, which then takes on its full meaning for the first time. Are we finally dealing with a piece of information, with a substance? No more than before. It is still not a matter of being conveyed via a few flights of stairs towards a remote reality, but of getting closer to a reality made more and more present by the speech this word gives rise to, now comprehensible to our ears through the renewal of the spirit. What was his name, this nameless one made present, the unprofferable finally revealed? Once again, explicitly, literally, piously, faithfully, humbly, the name says the thing at issue: 'I am [. . .] which is, and which was, and which is to come' [Revelation 1:8]. In other words, *always in other words*: the one who rises up once more, permanently present. Not unutterable through distancing, but through proximity. Too close, too intense to be looked in the face.

It'd be hard to be more precise, to capture more aptly the effect of this way of speaking that we call religious – at least in the tradition of which I would like to be able to say, without shame, that I'm the heir. No substance, no access, no mastery. Words that do what they say and are called, for this reason, sacramental. A presence that we are in constant danger of losing, that needs to be restated anew by the word that must be restated by the spirit that must be restated by us, yes, even by me, here, now – without which, the meaning would immediately be lost. The whole stratum, the whole chain, the whole procession must be deployed so that each of the elements makes sense. If 'God' was enough, what purpose would 'Jesus' and his preaching have served? If that preaching was enough, what good would the 'Spirit' have been? If the 'Spirit' was enough, why the 'Church' and its hard work of judgement? If the 'Church' was enough, why me, here, now, with my pathetic words? If I was sufficient to the task, what would you be doing here, reader? And the whole thing has to take off again, in the other direction, going from the present to the past: you must indeed finally begin to understand what I keep restating, which is nothing but the faithful repetition of the Church's inspired interpretation of holy words that allow us to understand what the 'Son of man' was saying when he renewed the sense of venerable expressions concerning the deeply moving presence of what his people then called 'God'. Nothing could be less mysterious, nothing less spectacular, nothing less abstruse than that big deal known as the 'Trinity'. It only becomes a real tangle if we try to tidy away substances whose sense has been lost; then, yes, it is in actual fact enough to tangle up the hypostases – the real substances of each of the three divisions of the Trinity. It isn't a mystery in the sense of an obscure message hidden from the common run of mortals but, yet again, the mystery of a *sequence*, a subtle sleight of hand, an extremely simple savoir-faire that draws out the reality in talk whose operating conditions alone allow us to speak properly. Yes, a gospel.

What? Is that all? Is that really enough to talk about these things again? How can I put it, honestly, without shocking both those on the inside and those on the outside: 'G. is just a manner of speaking; Jesus is just the word of G.; the Spirit is just a way of restating'? Don't those words verge on blasphemy? Haven't I taken away too much materiality, too much objectivity, too much substance, too much history from the things we're talking about? I've only just found the word again, and already I'm in danger of losing it straightaway. This is because my horses are too unstable, being required as they are to pull along together both the demand for reality and dependence on ways of speaking. How can we not be terrified of the difficulty of the enterprise? At the slightest hesitation on the part of the coach-man, those two animals part ways: reality goes off in one direction, speech in another. The first becomes too heavy, too material, too objective: it demands too much evidence; the second become too linguistic, too intellectual, too flimsy: it demands too much reflection, reflexivity. Yet, I know very well, there's no shortage of textual evidence: the only issue here is the Word. But we can no longer understand that expression, for we've turned this *logos* itself into a substance, one that has the strange particularity of being 'endowed with speech' to boot. Once the respective role of essence and attributes is reversed, the word *logos* no longer manages piously to preserve the sense of 'that which makes us talk properly' – which we can then, after the event, turn into a noun *or not*. How can we become realistic and objective again, while focusing our attention on the regime of utterance alone? Some want to 'preserve the treasure of faith' by clinging to a 'substantial God' and avoid everything going up in smoke; others want to make living relation-ships the sole rock on which to build religion, dodging

133

this corpse that slows down their progress. The first never stop accumulating 'objective proofs' to anchor their faith in enough historical evidence; the others never stop looking for 'symbolic meanings' to avoid getting trapped by misuse of reference.

Even though this particular schism seems irreparable, I don't have a choice: I have to remain the attentive coach driver, watching over these skittish horses that pull in opposite directions. Those on the inside feel religion would lack realism if we were to transform all these things into simple ways of speaking; those on the outside, conversely, think that there would be much too much vulgar realism if we were to start pointing to what the properly spoken, properly understood word does. The first are outraged at a speech requirement that seems to them to be marked with the stamp of relativism: 'Why not say, while you're at it, that the whole thing is just a pack of lies?' The second are outraged at a relativism that would end up, ultimately, rehabilitating the just and profound materiality of what they take to be a hotchpotch of poppycock accumulated over the course of history: 'Why not say, while you're at it, that the Holy Virgin truly appears in the course of her apparitions!' Yet, never has that incredibly hackneyed, misunderstood word, *relativism*, been more right than in the matter of religion: it speaks of relationship, scruples and contemplation as accurately as the word 'religion' itself whose various etymologies speak of the bringing into relationship, attachment, care and contemplation. But what relationship, what contemplation, what scruples? This is where we have to choose the type of reality, realism, objectivity, historicity that we want to revive: either the realistic but absent presence of a substance remote from us in time and space, rendered forever incomprehensible to our ears, insensitive to passing time, to the exactingness of the *ego, hic, nunc*; or the real presence of a word restated in these times and this place, and which depends entirely on current conditions of utterance. In the one case, time passes in vain, in vain do human beings speak; in the other, on the contrary, everything depends on human beings, time makes and breaks, proves and falsifies, presents and ruins. In the one case, there is no more relationship, no contemplation, or care; in the other, there are scruples, revival and attachment.

Is it enough to go from the realism of the substance to the realism of the relationship for the old buried words to retrieve their freshness, their clarity, their visibility? Let's try again. 'God is nobody' sounds strange to our ears; but if I say: 'The thing that turns us into individuals who are close and present might well, in certain places and in certain times, have been called "God", but we could also, today, just as easily call it by another vocable, such as "The thing that begets neighbours".' What's so shocking about that, either for the faithful or for the unfaithful? The 'non-existence of God' registers this evocation as precisely as the old expression 'God' – no, a lot more precisely actually, since it registers it *today, carefully, for me*, whereas the other expression registered it in days gone by for peoples forever remote in time: to keep trotting it out would consequently smack of *negligence*, speaking today as if 'God' existed. You don't put new wine into old wineskins [Luke 5:37].

'Eternal life' no longer makes any kind of sense,

especially for those who weep before the open graves where their loved ones lie. But if I say that in love everyone experiences a decisive, definitive kind of time that no longer passes in the mortal fashion of estrangement; that it is this kind of time that they should have held on to in their short lives if they had really loved their badly loved ones; that it is firstly for this that they shed bitter tears, for this loss of time, for all those wasted opportunities – have I lost something essential along the way? Yes, since I've lost the essence that made us direct our gaze towards the inaccessible beyond, as though we could imagine seeing again, later on, those we have forever lost; and no, since I've held on to the relationship which once more directs our attention, care, cautiousness towards what lies prone before us now, the love we so painfully regret not acting on in time. Eternity was yesterday and we didn't realize. The time is fulfilled; we've lived absently. In losing the substance, haven't I kept the essential? In keeping the substance, wouldn't I have lost its connectiveness, its being brought back into play? Who is more scrupulous? Who is more contemplative? Who is more realistic? Who is more objective?

So, one of two things: either we start from the substance and go on to the attributes, in which case we'll say that 'God exists', that he 'speaks', that he is 'the creator', 'all-powerful', 'merciful', 'eternal', 'our saviour' and so on; or we produce attributes that we then attach either to the expression 'God', when it is audible to the people we're addressing, or to any other expression that allows us to register it more faithfully for other peoples – those, say, for whom the 'non-existence of God' serves as an obvious and indisputable fact. It's as if there were (at least) two kinds of objectivity, two kinds of realism, one defined by obstinacy, the other by revival or a regathering of sense. The first comes down from the past to the future, time passes pointlessly in this form of realism or objectivity, since nothing of what exists, and nothing of what is uttered, can change the immutable substance that is expressed through its attributes; the other goes back from the present to the past, and everything depends on the capacity of the present event to replay the whole of history. The first case can't fail, the second, though, *can fail*: the whole difference lies there. The first is just the ineluctable realization of a plan determined in advance – give or take a few tweaks; the second is actual history, our history, the chips are not yet down. You have to choose. You can't speak religiously by jabbering away in both languages at once. Well, actually, you can, alas, we are always stuttering – especially me – since everything becomes false or everything becomes true according to the form of utterance; it all depends, and it all depends on us, yes, on me.

Nothing could be more crushing than the dogma known as the 'incarnation of God made man'. Recited *backwards*, diabolically, descending from the substance to the attributes, this tale warps into a tale of the supernatural, a gothic story of salvation for which there are no more listeners today, except for the believers in the fold: a 'God' 'will redeem' 'sinning mankind' by sending 'his only begotten Son' whose 'death on the cross', followed by the 'resurrection', is supposed to allow him to 'save' the world. Told this way, the story no longer has any truth value: it is neither true nor false; at best we

137

will turn it into an object of belief, at worst of mockery, since we can no longer see how to find its touchstone, its proofs, its verifiers, its authentifications, its guarantees; it's take it or leave it, swallow it whole or vomit it up just like that. But as soon as we put it back on its feet, by taking it *the right way round* again, starting from the attributes and going back (or not) to the substance, it becomes accurate again since it retrieves all its truth values: once again it is true or false, open to proof, to verification, guarantees, authentifications. Am I capable of speaking about something that is not remote but close, not spiritual but carnal, not dead but alive? And isn't the thing I speak about, the talking itself, capable of redressing those I address, to the point where the expressions 'saved', 'redeemed', 'resurrected' seem right again to them, even if nothing, nothing in the rest of their world has changed?

The lovers know very well that the talk that saves them from moving apart does not come from afar, but lives among them, it lifts their existence without actually changing it, it doesn't add one bit of information, no knowledge, not a single fact to their little world, yet it has already *transfigured* that world, from within. They know that it's not about moving apart by directing their gaze upwards to the heavens, to the spirit, but about coming closer by directing their talk downwards, to the body. And the proofs are as striking as they are incontestable: either I falsely utter the word 'incarnation' and nothing happens, or I utter it aptly and that word does what it says: it's now or never, it's you or no one, it's in this body or nowhere else. It speaks of urgency and alerts us to a presence that's there for all time, temporar-

ily permanent. Yes, 'the time is fulfilled' [Mark 1:15]. 'I
see, I am disabused.' No way out. What's more, at that
moment I understand, without really being surprised,
how in very ancient times Greek listeners registered
this stupefying experience by sinking deeper and deeper
and with great delight into the mazes of a metaphysics
about the 'true God/true man'. After all, no expression is better than any other; the innovations I have
to make repeatedly to spread this truth in other times
and in other places are neither worse nor better, since
only effective realization of what they incarnate can
provide them with their truth value, their index, their
stamp. These are sacramental words that oblige those
who utter them to do what they say – or to lie. Besides,
doesn't the dogma of the incarnation repeat, explicitly
and reflexively, how we are meant to understand the
efficacy specific to the word of salvation: a god was
made man, what was on high came down here below,
what was far away came near, what was absent is from
now on present? The truthfulness of the story depends
on the sequel, not on the beginning.

How derisory my translations are! How quickly
words which I think of as newly coined drop in value,
almost as soon as they're put into circulation! They
haven't managed to capture anything, to play back the
reality they were meant to record. There is something
disheartening, we must admit, about this dependence
of the word on the present day, on the current conditions of utterance. All the more so as all the efforts at
apologetics, over the course of time, have been directed
against that very dependence. Torrents of sermons,
thousands of volumes have been poured out to see to

it that the 'existence of God' does *not depend* on the word, on the will, on the goodwill of human beings. And, conversely, it is precisely the 'enemies of religion' who have, always, had a field day with this obvious fact: human beings make the gods in their own image. And now, I'm hoping to use relativism to reclaim that critical vocabulary to record religious speech piously and faithfully? Mankind, that god-making machine. It's insane. Or else, what we're dealing with here is an apologetics even more perverse than the rest, a cleric's ruse.

And yet, there is indeed something right and accurate in this expression: 'The existence of G. now depends on us.' In this whole business, isn't it a question, literally, piously, ritually, of a 'God' that man – that a woman – has begotten? Didn't that woman have to trot out judiciously these few words of acceptance: 'Behold the handmaid of the Lord'? [Luke 1:38]. The lovers know very well that the presence of their love depends on the way they talk to each other anew to make each other present for the other, so why couldn't we make good use of the same thing? They don't rely on assurance of their affection, on its force of inertia, either; and yet, when they finally come to love each other, it would never occur to them to attribute their salvation to their own resources – they wouldn't be so silly. On the contrary, it is only in the estrangement phase, in the middle of the crisis, when they feel suffocated by the deadly weight of time, that they're reduced to their crafty manoeuvres alone. It's when they're incapable of getting themselves out of the hole they've fallen into that they solemnly implore assistance: 'Our love, come to our rescue!' – all the while knowing that no one will come and support them and that they're as incapable of redeeming themselves as Baron Munchausen. So the lovers clearly take themselves to be the only possible artisans crafting their relationship, all the while knowing that they only become its exclusive makers in the living hell of estrangement: once they're close again, they recognize with absolute certainty that they have been *made by* the love that finally came to their aid.

Is it really indispensable to being able to talk about religion for us to go back over the horrible difficulties of that little verb: 'to make'? Alas, yes. Nothing has blown out the translation arrears like this suicidal battle against the discourse of those who turned religion into a 'simple man-made thing'. But we should have done the opposite and welcomed them with open arms! Yes, canonize Voltaire, Feuerbach, Nietzsche, Marx, Freud, declare them Fathers of the Church. St Friedrich would have been more help to us than praying to Bernadette Soubirous in Lourdes, and his sanctuary at Sils-Maria would not have given rise to any fewer miracles (only in China can you see chapels, inside temples, dedicated to philosopher saints). At the very moment when we should have folded our tents and left the old world behind, filled as it was with a 'helpful God' to whom you addressed prayers, the Apocryphal Fathers were familiarizing us with a world not emptied of 'God', but, on the contrary, *filled* with his existence. They did for their venerable beliefs the same work of translation and revival that their ancestors had done for the naiads, sylphs and gods of Olympus. How could the history of religious utterance stop at any particular form of recording, when care and scruple demand that we speak of the actual presence of

141

whatever must, for us, at that instant, be represented? How can we tell in advance if the expression 'man makes his gods' will register this presence any less potently than 'a God made man', an age-old vocable that has become inaudible for many? The thing that made the ancient divine idiom so convenient is that no one saw the slightest problem with it: in what tongue should we speak of G. today to get back that same sense of obvious fact? If at Pentecost they once used to speak Parthian, Greek and Syriac, why couldn't we have spoken Freud, Feuerbach or Renan? What were you so afraid of? What was this treasure that, to be preserved, had never to be spent? Don't you know the fate in store for hoarders? What good to you is amassing fortunes of faithfulness, if you can't take a penny of it with you into the present time in which you have to love and speak?

So, if I want to hold in one hand both the objectivity of the beings produced by religion and their dependence on speech acts, I would have to have at my disposal a sense of the word 'to make' that is not critical. That's the only way we could uncover the original mechanism behind those immense strata of discourses, inventions, elaborations, behind all that labour, all those defects, all those setbacks of faithfulness without actually taking away an ounce of reality from them, without ever letting them become outdated. Well, I can no longer use that word 'making' positively, but I really need it if I'm to continue. Thanks to the battle against religion, it has become synonymous with falseness. Why? Because, to the humble and honest work of making, they've surreptitiously added a crazy hypothesis about the craftsman's domination of his œuvre.

Who has ever seen a builder actually master his building? Where is the creator who feels himself capable of controlling his creature? What robotician thinks he's the master of his robots, what marionettist isn't taught amazing tricks by his marionettes? By revealing the secrets behind the making of gods, the new Church Fathers did us all a mighty service, since it's only after achieving mastery, basically, that they got any guts: there is no master at all. Yes, most exactly: 'Neither God nor master'. But the clerics were frightened that, if human beings were granted the capacity to make their divinities, they would take all the power of mastery and set themselves up in the place of 'God'. Well, that place does not exist. The notion of making in no way entails that of an all-powerful maker. Only the ancient world had an omnipotent creator to whom you could actually imagine giving a successor called 'mankind'. But earthlings? Mortals? Us? You? Me? Where do you see masters, emperors, controllers? There is no mastery. You who are on the inside, this world terrifies you because, according to you, it's 'without a divine master'. But don't you see that it's also *without a human master*? You who are on the outside, this call for renewal of 'God' horrifies you because, according to you, it would bring back the old tyranny of the divine. Don't you see that this world is forever *without a creator*?

The clerics thought they had to base their sermons on the weakness of man, even daring to find in his lapses a proof of the grandeur of their 'Lord'. Think of the sermons they might have given if they, like the Apocryphal Fathers, had instead invoked the weakness, the passivity, the dependency of G.! Instead of fighting against that mysticism, 'atheism', wouldn't they have done better to rejoice in a world at last delivered from the poison of mastery? And, conversely, you humanists, instead of pitting respect for man against the barbarity of religions, wouldn't you have done better to find the antidotes to disintoxicate yourselves from the hard drug of control? Do you all really believe that history ought to amount to no more than a playground seesaw whereby 'God' only rises as far as the human being is lowered; where Man only triumphs if 'God' dies? Times change. The face of the earth has long been renewed. There is no control and no all-powerful creator, either – no more 'God' than man – but there is care, scruple, cautiousness, attention, contemplation, hesitation and revival. To understand each other, all we have is what comes from our own hands, but that doesn't mean our hands can be taken for the origin.

There's no way I can talk about these things if I can't recover the capacity to make the truth, to express reality. I have to be able to talk about religious elaboration without threatening voices, coming from inside as much as outside, immediately asking me to choose: 'Is it real or is it made up?' I have to be able to answer once more: 'Both'. And for my adversaries, as much as those who think they understand me, not to conclude that I'm taking refuge by so replying in the cynical illusion of an idol-maker attributing to the products of his hands the reality he has projected on to them.

Obviously, I'm never going to get out of this one. I'm never going to be able to resume speaking since I also lack the capacity to reconnect language and reality. It's as if I'd been stripped of the right to employ this gesture

144

of making, of constructing, of elaborating, of relating, that can express the real *for real*, without immediately being accused of naivety, cynicism or bad faith. I no longer own any of those words capable of doing what they say: 'rituals', 'sacraments', 'sermons'. It's as if religious utterance had stripped itself of all the material and practical means of making the good word, as if it had, with its own hands, smashed the word-mill, the prayer-mill. What's more, this is hardly surprising, since the sciences themselves, in the days of modernism, also forgot how you used to be able to 'make objective truth'. It was then that they agreed to let themselves be betrayed by double-click communication with its absurd claim to the existence of a truth 'not made by human hand', *acheiropoieta* . . .

If all I had against me was the inevitable wear and tear of words slipping from the present towards the past, I'd extricate myself; if all I had against me was the long history of anti-religion, I'd cope without too much trouble; if all I had against me were the traps of apologetics and rationalization, I'd manage to outsmart them. But I also have against me what the friends of religion, as much as their unrelenting enemies, agree on taking as the supreme virtue: hatred of idols.

Who can measure the biting irony of this paradox? The religious, like their enemies, have been vying with each other to see who can knock down the greatest number of fetishes, denounce false gods the most fiercely. They decided it was their duty not to *be taken in* by the ungodly mix of fabrication and reality shown, according to them, by the fetish-makers. The former believed you had to avoid confusing belief in 'one God' with the

horrible confusion of false gods; the latter thought you
had to avoid confusing trust in 'one Reason' with the
archaic belief in a 'God' who'd become one chimera
among other chimeras. The thing that hasn't changed
throughout this stream of mistaken identities is the arm
of the iconoclast bearing a hammer – or the burning flare
that he holds to the stake. According to the religious, as
much as to their enemies, what you had to avoid at all
costs was taking what could 'only' be the result of our
human labour for an independent reality. And there's
nothing new about that: legend has it that Abraham,
father of three religions, launched his brilliant career
by wrecking the humble idol shop kept by his father,
Terah. Since that founding gesture, destructive and critical as it was, wanton destruction has been perpetuated
in one continual fire, incessant carnage, a piety that
doesn't know how else to manifest itself except by an
ever-renewed sacrifice of taboos, idols, images, dogmas,
fetishes, golden calves and false gods. Above all, they
say, do not believe, do not let yourself *be taken in*, don't
let yourself *be had*, don't let yourself *be conned*.

And yet, what proof do we have that this war against
idols was actually necessary? Why should we prolong
it ad nauseam today? Of course, in the days when the
'gods' formed an indisputable framework for daily
existence, it was indeed necessary to set up a jealous
'God', to knock over all his rivals' altars. But how can
this ancient and venerable war still matter to us, when
we take the non-existence of the gods to be the indisputable framework of our fragile lives? In believing that
our religious duty demanded the smashing of fetishes,
idols and taboos, we have inadvertently stomped on

146

something quite different: one of the springs of the action that in actual fact allowed us to make realities independent of us, without lying. By knocking over the altars of false gods, we have plunged humanity into obscurity, since we've forced ourselves to believe that their makers naively and falsely believed in them. By the same token, we've peopled the world with barbarians, with manipulators and the manipulated. Through a stupefying reversal, it is we the enlighteners who have produced obscurity and we the unbelievers who have everywhere generated blind belief. In effect, to explain the attachment of idolaters and fetishists to their idols when, according to us, they couldn't not be aware that they were their *sole* craftsmen, we have believed that *they must have believed*, that they were had by their own production. We have imagined that they attributed an autonomous reality to what they themselves had constructed, which is strictly true, but not in the sense the critics mean: the œuvre of our hands knows, sometimes, in fact, how to produce, record, reveal, evoke what possesses us. 'These idols have eyes and see not, ears and hear not, hands and touch not', we said, mockingly, without seeing to what extent it was we ourselves that this malediction condemned. Yes, it does in fact condemn us, strictly accurately, strictly precisely: we, the smashers of idols, we have eyes and see not, ears and hear not, hands incapable of touching – except to deconstruct, to criticize and smash. The hammer of radical criticism has bounced back; it's us that it's hit in the head; we're still stupid and stunned from the blow.

You're joking! You don't mean to say that to talk about religion again we have to revert to idols, put back up the altars to the false gods, once more embrace poly-theism, sacrifice to fetishes, and not just swallow the preposterous tall tales of clerics anymore but also the hideous fantasies of their most mortal enemies: wizards, charlatans, magicians? How can we accept, without risk, going back on the obvious facts common both to the great religions and to the official rationalisms which derived directly from them? Surely you aren't claim-ing to take relativism that far? Otherwise, what you're inviting us to is no longer the rebooting of religious utterance, but a Faustian pact which all that remains to us of virtue would rebel against.

And yet, here too, there has also been a category mistake, as if in speaking of an event capable of pro-ducing close and present individuals, we'd confused it with *another* battle, one that's incidental and now superfluous, even dangerous. As if we'd had trouble, at first, *freeing* religious utterance from another kind that would generate other goals, other truths, other realities, and in relation to which it is now completely superfluous to squabble. What harm can fetishes do to anyone who seeks to get closer to coming together, to representation? How can idols, domestic, cultural or civic, upset those who form a virtual people of the saved and the newly close who elude all borders? Why would what consoles and heals through the subtle barter of sacrifice, entreaty and prayer upset anyone who seeks presence and sal-vation? Angels can get about perfectly comfortably without actually disturbing demons. Especially if the faithful can only go on speaking properly of their G. by resorting to the *same mechanisms* as those whose altars they brought down. They, too, must make with their

148

own hands *icons* in place of the *idols* brought down, and these icons, too, must become genuine. In destroying the idols, the anti-fetishists forgot that they were making forever incomprehensible the icons necessary to the public exercise of their word and their worship. In smashing the idols, they tied their hands in an impossible *double bind*, since they still insist on making a reality while depriving themselves of the humble means of producing it. Isn't that the source of the fanaticism generated by the religions known as being of the Book? The origin of this sudden alternation between an absolutely free 'God' dominating an altogether powerless human being, and a human being who is sole master of completely fabricated gods, weeping in pity over his all-powerlessness? In believing they were *doing right*, first the religious, and then the anti-religious, deprived themselves of any possibility of *making well*? There is no paradox here, but a very simple, obvious fact: how could those who need *iconophilia* to manage still to speak properly of their faith inherit the iconoclast tradition, without the benefit of an inventory? If the real presence of G. in the talk that has a bearing on him depends on that talk itself, what madness to sever with the stroke of a sword the link that ties human practice and autonomous reality!

We must have lost our way somewhere, since iconoclasm now triumphs, the critical spirit reigns alone and we can no longer reconcile the two expressions: 'It's true, it's manufactured.' Unless we understand it *a minima* as the simple projection of an illusion onto the mute, blank screen of the clouds that bad faith alone can make us 'take for' a consistent reality. Well, those who

149

are accused, most wrongly, of naively believing in their fetishes have in fact preserved this precious savoir-faire: they can say in the same breath and without trembling that they made with their own hands the thing that nonetheless saves them and gives them life, that possesses them and holds them. Who can paint an icon today and say, in good faith, that it is acheiropoietic? And yet it is an obvious, everyday fact that lovers go through without feeling the merest hint of the slightest contradiction: yes, they are the ones speaking and they depend only on themselves; yes, it is indeed their love that has shaped them and pulled them out of the hole in which they were languishing in isolation. That particular conduit – are we still allowed to take it, trembling in terror? Can you be a constructivist, meaning a realist, when it comes to religion the way you can be (as I learned) in the sciences? Can I now forget about the comminatory question: 'Is it real or is it made?' and, here too, substitute the question: 'How do you tell the difference between what is *well* and what is *badly* made?'

Frankly, it's hard to see why he persists. He will never be able to talk about these things again. He has to fight against too many habits, too many reflexes, pay off too many arrears. That's not a bullock sitting on his tongue, not letting him speak, but a whole herd of mad cows. It's too complicated if he has to revive everything again, from the definition of 'God' right down to the definition of amorous talk, via the very concept of the making of idols – not to mention the appalling complications that consist of lying, rationalization, translation and revival in which he has floundered around so happily. The

logical solution ought to be the reverse of the one he
has come up with till now: whatever you do, don't talk
about these things again; let them roll back the stone
over the tomb of religion and bury it once and for all; let
them talk no more of the living dead who came to suck
our blood; let them drive a nice sharp stake between their
ribs. *Vade retro, satanas.* [Get thee behind me, Satan!]
The solution of his contemporaries and peers is excel-
lent; he should have started with that; he would have
spared himself quite a lot of trouble: religion is finished.
It only offers archaic consolations, an irrational residue,
a pathetic effort to put up barriers in the face of the non-
sense of existence, a child's drawing coloured in to put
a bit of colour and warmth into the colourless world of
cold reason. Of course, religion still offers a subject for
study, we can still look into the enthusiasms it stirs up,
but there's nothing living, essential about it any more,
nothing in any case that ought to take up intellectual
space, at least not in our comfortable climates; it long
ago left the realm of health and entered pathology, even
teratology. He's not the one who's going to extricate it
from that. And anyway, who'd want to give place and
weight again to the ravings of retards, bigots, sancti-
monious hypocrites, inquisitors and fanatics? *Ecrelinf*,
Voltaire was right to finish his letters with this cruel
invocation: *Ecrasons l'infâme*, 'Let us crush the vile.'

Yes, everything in religion is false; and yet everything
is true, down to the last comma. Like those anamor-
phoses, so popular in the classical age, which all at
once transform some monstrous daub into a painting as
clear as day, as long as you look at the right spot at the
right angle. I can't overcome this hesitation, which has

nothing to do with swinging indecisively between unbelief and belief, between 'I spit it all out' and 'I swallow it all hook, line and sinker.' Hesitation is the thing itself, always to be revived and reformulated. Nothing to do with some stupid wager about the respective chances of a long-term coup – though one with spectacular gains, 'eternity'! – as against the infinitesimal stakes of small-time gambling. I'm looking for the exact opposite of that grotesque apologetics: either I get closer to the present, to what is lying in front of me; or I move away for good and turn towards the thick cloud cover. Is it my fault if, through a translation deficit, the sense of the religious has been reversed to the point of designating the distant instead of the near, the absent instead of the present, the spirit instead of the flesh, the next world instead of this world, the transcendent instead of the immanent? Can we still, today, reverse this reversal and put back on its feet what has been walking on its head? On the one hand, everything is so heavy, it's hopeless; on the other, everything is light, it's really very simple, a child of seven would get it without any trouble. Yes, I'm right to hesitate, right to persist. I've gone to too much trouble. I want to get my inheritance back. Now is absolutely not the time to let go. The worst is behind me.

Till now, I've talked about religion in the interests of speed, but there is no essence of the religious, nothing that allows us to designate such diverse forms of life using the same term. If so many people reach for their guns whenever they hear talk of a 'return to religion', this is because they expect to see the return of the old amalgam that mixed up peoples, administrations, moral

codes, economies, laws – in short, a total and often total-
itarian life-form – in the search for a complete world, a
harmonious cosmos that demanded that it satisfy them
completely, without any gaps and without any residues,
without any cracks and without any opposition. That
world, of course, will not come again; if certain people
still admire it, they do so as aesthetes. You might as well
try to get steam trains running again beside the high-
speed rail lines or beribboned oxcarts along pilgrimage
routes. We can engage in these reconstructions for the
benefit of tourists desperate for a bit of cultural heritage, but nothing active, alive, indispensable will happen
anymore in these customs forever made irrelevant. And
so much the better, for all the work of history was
needed to bring out bit by bit the tonality specific to
religious utterance – something which it long, too long,
confused with the political, moral, sexual, ethnic, legal,
artistic, customary requirements via which it was able to
express itself for a time, but which isn't up *to registering*
forever the one thing at issue: its good word. The real
betrayal on the part of the clergy, the thing that makes
them so incapable of defending themselves against the
accusation of archaism, is not having seen this slow
and gradual *disinterment* as an opportunity offered to
recover their freedom of speech. At last, religion could
stand on its own two feet, without aiming for a thousand interfering goals that other language games, other
utterances achieved much better than it did. No world is
preferable to ours, to this one, to the only one we have,
if we're going to talk about religion, since, by definition, it is to this present world and in its own language
that we need to address ourselves if we want the words

of the tradition to resound anew in a truthful way. To wait until we find ourselves transported miraculously to other times and places in order to speak truly is, by design, to lie.

We must, then, proceed in reverse: not to compare all that has been called religion throughout the ages so as to extract the bone marrow, the common standard, the yardstick, but conversely, to find out how, given the particular demands of this regime of utterance, it could serve as a touchstone for judging the presence or absence of the religious in the other life-forms. How can we distinguish good manufacturing from bad, the good elaboration from the bad? But all the things this test ends up rejecting won't be convicted of falseness, of lying, of heresy or impiety; they simply belong to other forms of truth, other regimes of speech yet to be defined.

Let's do this thought experiment: let's withdraw religious utterance as I've defined it from the world. What would happen? By reducing religion to its simplest expression, you could just say that, without it, *there would be nobody anymore*. Everything would remain in place: nations, societies, persons, worlds, assemblies, collectives, regulations, economies, cosmologies, divinities; the only thing missing would be the making of persons made close because they've been gripped by a form of temporality that no longer goes from the past to the present, but the other way round, from the present to the whole of the past and the future. In this limited, terribly limited, sense, demanding to live without religion would come down, in the eyes of that tradition, to living *with no presence and with nobody*, like the living dead. Lovers know very well that their love is not their whole life: that they work, they desire, they go about all kinds of business; but they would surely not agree to deprive themselves of being brought close together again thanks to the so very original, so very originating words that they call 'their love' and that do what they say. If questioned, they would no doubt say that their love is 'the meaning of their life', even if they immediately allowed that this meaning comes on top of a hundred others which they also value but with which it couldn't be confused. Similarly, religion can't sum up all modes of existence – the old mistake was to have tried to use it like a cope to encompass the whole sum of life-forms – but it *adds* its own tonality, without which there would be no neighbours made present to each other, without which the time would never be fulfilled, without which history would pass in vain, without which death would triumph.

But that's not enough! This definition is far too limited to satisfy the appetite of the religious. You're only giving them just enough to live on. They'll never be satisfied with so little. They want everything, the cosmos, history, everyday life, morality, art, architecture, the lot, even our most intimate inner secrets – this world below as well as the otherworld. It really wasn't worth the trouble of rejecting the help of purification, if it was just to translate the whole vast sum of religious elaboration into the pathetic gobbledegook of 'the making of individuals made close again'. Either religion is truthful and it extends everywhere, or it is untruthful and it shouldn't be granted anything, not even the presence of individuals. All you're offering us here is a lame compromise which will shock the faithful every bit as much as the unfaithful, those on the inside as much as those on the outside. What a bad diplomat you make. This is even worse than reducing the Word to a simple 'way of speaking'.

There's nothing I can do about it. To find the right words again you have to use whatever speaks to the ears of those you're addressing. I don't in any way claim that the minuscule layer of meaning I'm clinging to has any kind of privilege, that it might serve as a metalanguage for translating the immense corpus of religious sentiment in its entirety. There is no good metalanguage, as we well know, no standard, no yardstick: the most mawkish phrases or the most elaborate, the most venerable or the newest, the most moving or the coldest become equally right or untruthful according to their sole capacity to make what they are talking about, in the instant, for whoever hears them. The felicity conditions, the tone, the tonality and the rhythm are *almost* completely independent of the form employed, since what matters is something else entirely which points to itself obliquely, through the discrepancies, the implausible details, the cracks in the message. In religion, as in tone, anything goes. But if there is no right metalanguage, there is no bad or inappropriate metalanguage, either. The only question is one of knowing how we can *discern* the quality of the utterance and then, thanks to this critical discernment – yes, critical, logical and even rational in its way – link up with all the other layers of meaning thanks to which other persons, who've become members of the same people, have tried, in other times and places, to express the same thing in different rituals. The issue is not one of knowing if you need to please the religious or not, to flatter the unfaithful or not, but whether, in distinguishing good translations from bad, you can draw the virtual people again, that 'communion of saints', made up of those who retrospectively understand the buried truth of words revived in the mouths of the living – for it's the living we're dealing with, not the dead. This is the only touchstone, the only occasion when that 'everything is true' tips over into 'everything is false', or not – yes, the only *kairos*.

If my efforts at translation seem so derisory, that is because I've used the only form of speech that is still available and fresh despite the dizzying debts of arrears: the speech of love, of the *presents* the lovers give each other when they can't, or no longer really want to, calculate. Naturally, the impression remains of an infinite abyss between the small joys and small miseries of personal love and the great passions and great crimes of public religions. Even though the anonymous authors of the Gospels known as 'the Infancy Narratives' also set up the same short-circuit between the humble business of human affection and the grandiose scenographies of biblical history, we can no longer see how to get from one to the other just through the synonymy of that most inane of words: 'love'. Yet, the capacities for discrimination offered by the lovers' crisis are not negligible. We know in our bones – every one of us slowly does their apprenticeship in this, against his or her will – all the registers of lying, bad faith, avoidance, flight, reconciliation and forgiveness. How many hours do we spend developing this savoir-faire, choosing our touchstones, refining our taste? There's nothing private, personal, individual in these skills. No institution is vaster, more

157

widespread, more imperious, more tyrannical at times than that of amorous speech. It needs all the resources of Hollywood, the 'sacred grove' of California, all the output of novels, the whole romance press described so aptly, in French, as 'of the heart', hundreds of hours of phoning, scores of experiences, of ruptures, of advice, of effusions, of confidences, to learn how to make out, in all the confusion of passion, the delicate path of salutary words that rally or destroy, reinvigorate or kill, bring closer or distance forever. Yet we're supposed to deprive ourselves of this model, this template, this mould? We're supposed to turn it into some sort of inner, psychological thing, when it is obviously a robust and fruitful institution, riddled with heresies and revolts, scandals and revolutions, gnawed away by doubt, bombarded by a torrent of opinion, advice, discourse, reforms, disciplines and pontification. Who would have learned to love if he hadn't been taught these hosts of contradictory ways of doing so? Nothing could be less spontaneous, individual, autonomous than these particular forms of discernment.

The thing that makes recourse to the public institution of amorous speech so incongruous as a means of restoring a taste for religious language is not only the immense difference in scale between the psychological and the cosmic, the individual and the collective; it is not only that the former still speaks to our contemporaries whereas the latter no longer convinces any but the greatest believers, those in the fold. It is that amorous discourse can seem to us *at once* alive and institutionalized, universal and controversial, whereas, for the latter, age-old religious speech, we always feel like we have to *separate* life and the institution, the personal and the universal, the free and the forced.

Ah, the institution! The only real scapegoat of the past century. It's always described as tyrannical, archaic, old-hat, domineering, suffocating, castrating, hierarchical, obsolete, sterile, legalistic, formalistic . . . There aren't many contemporaries who haven't tried to tear them-selves free of it in order finally to 'get back' the freedom, fruitfulness, initiative, drive, authenticity of the mind. If, to start speaking again, all you had to do was avoid the traps of rationalization, climb back up the slope of pass-ing time, pay back the debts of our predecessors; if all you had to do was fight the reflexes of anti-fetishism, we might be capable of it, but then, we'd still have to shake off our mortal hatred for institutions. Along with criti-cal thinking, the desire not to be had, the war on naive belief, this prejudice forms the greater part of our intel-lectual virtues. Everything is upside down in this whole business of religion: to speak within it unimpeded, we have to chuck out what we take to be our most precious virtues.

But I don't have a choice. I know very well that no one can invent a language on his own, by himself, unless it's the language of madness, and that will get him locked up. There's no such thing as a private religion, a religion of one's own, anymore than there's such a thing as individual love: we have nothing at our disposal but the words of the tribe. If that. If lovers, curled up within the spring tide of public speech, can invent a code of their own composed of tiny rituals, keys, flowers and abracadabras known to themselves alone, no one can claim to speak the venerable language of religion once more, without a warrant and without backup, without the possibility of an appeal and without a vocation. It's not a matter anymore of merely forming a couple, a group, a family or a commune, but of gathering a new people together. Looking at it that way, of course, I've failed, I'm well aware, since, with my pathetic efforts to rearticulate the old vocabulary, I have no practical means of discerning their faithfulness, of sorting the good expressions from the bad, of deciding with others whether they are heretical or orthodox fabrications. All I have left are the ravings of a voice crying in the wilderness, which, if they could hear it, would probably scandalize those on the inside as much as those on the outside. By definition, I lack the collective capacity of discrimination.

But then, why not breach the institution and try to enter into *direct* contact with 'God'? Because there is no 'God', access leads anywhere but to him, the adjective 'direct' makes no sense in these matters. It's always tangentially, together, through the cross-ties of an impure, invented language that we finally find the words, those rare words that bring about what they say and that connect us, through the retrospective movement of this spirit of renewal, to what our predecessors tried to say. Escape is as impossible as purification, we'd lose even faster the treasure we hope to find on our own. No pidgin, no creole is the work of any one individual: to mangle the official language, you need to have cohabited for many a long year in the margins of a people who refuse you access to its master language. No, clearly, far from extricating yourself from the institution, you have to plunge into it; far from purifying speech, you have to learn to mill again a bit of the inappropriate that is nonetheless truthful. As the saying goes – the most inaudible of all sayings, the most despised, the most hated, the most unspeakable and the most scandalous, one that is barely out when it forces us to rinse our mouths: 'Outside the Church, there is no salvation.'

And yet no formula is more accurate, rational, precise, technical: no other touchstone exists to judge the quality of these strata of untruthful words, invented in their entirety, elaborated, revived, codified, reformed, rejected, revived, renewed, re-elaborated, abandoned, deformed, crushed, sedimented, reanimated, buried, twisted, lifted up, than the collective labour of those who recognize each other at times as forming part of the same virtual people – a people immediately torn apart, scattered, rebelling, unfaithful, ignorant, before it rallies again, reassembles, reconverts, recognizes itself again as a single and same sacred nation, before losing themselves a bit later in the sands of history. That's precisely because we can't expect any salvation *above and beyond* these thrusting sedimentary strata, because there is no other abode in which to talk of religion. There is no G. that is not this very labour of revival and evaluation, reform and straying, the very passing of the word through this great virtual and indistinct people. No revelation will ever be superior to this groping of the blind holding on to each other's shoulder to make progress in the dark. Those who've tried to do better, the cranks, have always done worse.

You might detest courts, councils, committees, bulls and being kept in line by a bishop's crosier, but we really have to find other procedures, other gatherings,

161

other magisteria, other sanctions to resume anew the same work of sorting out inventions precisely because there is nothing above, nothing transcendent, nothing higher, no court of appeal, no last word, no revelation, no dazzling bolt from the clouds that would allow us 'to tell the truth' *on top of* the slow collective and institutionalized discernment of truthful speech. You can abhor the pretensions of a clan, a sect, a Church, a religion with a universal empire, but then you'd need to discover other conduits, other interpreters, other orderings, other conclaves so as to form this virtual people who see themselves as closely bound in the same presence, contemporary with the same event, united by the same revelation of Scriptures till then obscure. Maybe we were wrong about the meaning of that monstrous saying in the name of which so many crimes were committed, so many stakes lit, so many crusades preached, but it remains no less true that *it has no opposite* since, by definition, what we call 'salvation' can only happen by tapping into those strata of words that are all untruthful, by rediscovering for ourselves what makes them all apt. The Church does better than being the incontestable repository of the truth: it is the *contested* repository of lies, elaborations, selections, revivals. It is on its machine for producing and discriminating that we need to learn to make connections. Well, this rediscovery can't be made by yourself, but only in a group – a group that itself endlessly changes circumference, encompassing the whole world or dwindling to nothing according to the intensity with which it rediscovers the message. It's precisely because we can't simplify the exercise of religious utterance that it's impossible to leap, in some dizzying bound, in some *salto mortale*, outside the institution, mortal and militant, fabricating and sinning, lying and falsifying, constructive and inventive as it is. Just as, outside the complex and fractionated institution of amorous discourse, no one would know how to talk about love.

Clearly, the list of ills that make it impossible to talk about religion again is growing. No wonder I held my tongue for so long.

We'd need firstly not to believe in belief; well, just about everybody approaches 'the issue of religion' by firmly asserting that it's a good idea to believe or not to believe.

We'd need then to give back some strength to the notion of construction, of fabrication; now just about all religious people and their enemies find themselves agreeing to pit what is real, objective, authentic, historic against what is artificial, invented, fabricated: you'd think the truth, for all of them, consisted in worshipping some image 'not made by human hand'.

Thirdly, we'd have to make the institution synonymous with innovation, whereas almost all our contemporaries assert that the weight of the institution and creative freedom are as opposed as fire and water.

We'd need, fourthly, to abandon anti-idolatry, even though the battle against fetishes forms the stock in trade of all critical thinking, that is to say, the only thing left when you've abandoned all thought.

We'd need, fifthly, to rehabilitate relativism to turn it into a spiritual virtue par excellence, but only the battle against relativism mobilizes believers and unbelievers, rationalists and irrationalists, progressives and reactionaries alike. You'd think they all preferred the absolute.

We should never have been modern – that way, we'd no longer link religion either with the archaic or with the modernization front; but, alas, we only ever talk about a religion 'torn between modernity and tradition'.

Lastly, we'd have to renew the holy words individually, whereas, by definition, there is no individual religion, and it's the whole people of the redeemed who must follow.

So, that's it, at least I've done my job, I've drawn up the estimate without hiding anything: that is the price we'd have to pay if we really wanted to rebuild the monuments of faith.

In which case it really is hopeless. No one will ever, consequently, speak the language of religion again. Suspended for a moment, the colossal debt of the translation arrears is presented to him once again to be paid in full – and he doesn't have a penny with which to settle it. How can you move the tongue in your mouth if, at every word, you have to shift the frightening weight of thousands of years of collective elaborations, most of which weigh as much as a sedimentary basin on a fern from the Carboniferous? Crushed, suffocated, fossilized, he has nothing left to say. He ought to have known, he was warned: all he had to do was not launch himself into this venture, which was lost before it began, into this last stand. The institution of religion will never recover the stature and drive that it would have held on to if every morning, throughout history, it had paid the price for the translation it needed to make it comprehensible and salutary for each of its new interlocutors.

To stop the truth from being merely relative – in Pontius Pilate's sense – they forgot along the way to make it relative to the language of those who were supposed to hear it. How can we retrace our footsteps in the opposite direction and so go from this standard, which is immutable and everywhere the same, to that other universal, which is everywhere different – yes, relative – thanks to which diverse peoples finally *realize* that they are linked by the same history, that in reality they form the same people, because they once more hear the same message in formulae that are all completely different? It's not possible. Lost time can't be regained.

All the more so as the temptation is great, in periods of backward surges, to repatriate the holy people to the shelter of borders that are a bit firm. To spare ourselves the demanding work of faithfulness, we rely on the robust pillars of politics and customs, on the old heavy inertia of habits and cultural affiliations. The virtual people of variable geometry then becomes a real people of an ever more limited surface area. The word 'faithfulness' no longer means that which revives the age-old message anew for other ears, but that which puts the minds of those in the fold to rest by rehashing the old words their childhood was lulled by. From that moment, there is an inside and an outside, a fortress besieged where the 'treasure of faith' is preciously preserved against the 'rising tide of barbarians'.

Yet, there is no resemblance between politics and religion, except for the homonyms 'people', 'composition' and 'representation'. Everything else is different, all the mechanisms, all the forms of speech, all the regimes of utterance. The people made up of the redeemed doesn't match up with the people made up of citizens. Both are well represented, but the sense of the word 'representation' is completely different. There is nothing in common between the person who finds himself deeply moved by the fulfilment of time that grips him once and for all and the person who is amazed to see that the order he receives from on high is also what he would have decided if he'd felt like it all by himself. The paths of salvation and those of freedom only meet at very infrequent junctions. We can't respect anew the delicate form of political speech except by carefully distinguishing it from the religious translation. By supporting one another clumsily, to spare ourselves the hard labour both of political revival and of religious revival, politicians and clerics have lost legitimacy every bit as much as discernment. That is why, between the virtual catholicity of a people to be resurrected and the narrow conduits of a Church both Roman and Catholic, there is now the whole impassable abyss of times laid waste, opportunities missed, nations abandoned, all the quarrels over rites lost by those who thought they'd won them. The jig's up. The death knell has sounded.

Unless there is more than one way to be faithful. Sometimes, on buildings bordering meandering rivers, you can see one of those carved high-water marks that recall hundred-year-old floods, marks that the current riverbed, calm and tame, doesn't look as if it could ever rise to again: there is faithfulness in those signs, which don't go down as far as the low-water mark but obstinately maintain the old level, for they help the passerby remember the power of still waters. I, too, have thought that it was more useful to draw one of those landmarks well away from the current course of the river so as to be able to measure, through letters written on a wall, the distance separating the present riverbed from future rises in water level. I've felt that I would thereby be more faithful than if I'd added the present low-water level or if I'd left the river valley for good to its twists and turns.

Yes, it's true, I've apparently located religious utterance well away from what is called religion, the Christian religion, the Catholic religion. I've stuck it in a particular agony of speech, in a specific hesitation, my own, thinking it was better to approach the machine for elaborating utterances, rather than commenting yet again on phrases whose mechanism today escapes the great majority. Even though everything in those utterances is false, everything becomes true if you translate them, if you transfer them while offering them the vehicle specific to them, which is not a message, a doctrine, an insight, a consolation, but a form of good word that does what it says: 'Look out! Get up, time is fulfilled, it's you I'm talking to, you are what it's about, here and now.' Either those phrases are heard and actually do what they say – and they are right – or they fail in their felicity conditions and they instantly become untruthful. Yes, a simple way of speaking known as 'the Word'. Is that enough to recover freedom of speech?

It's not enough, naturally, for this formulation refuses to choose between immanence and transcendence. Yet, it's not my fault if the distinction between this world and the next registers what it's all about so badly. The experience of a time from now on fulfilled comes and in fact *disrupts* the usual, habitual, deadly course of action

167

– lovers are well aware of this. And yet, this disruption doesn't distance us from passing time, from this world below, in order to sweep us away towards another realm, another time, but on the contrary, in order to bring us closer to this particular time, which is then fulfilled. So much so that, all in all, the term 'immanence' finally better describes the direction that this type of religious speech takes us in than the term 'transcendence', which gets lost in too many far distances. What is left of this age-old and venerable opposition between the two terms is the radical rupture, the obligatory conversion, the *kairos*, but the opposition between one world and another no longer registers anything essential. So, if we wanted to talk the language of religion again (but who wants to and, more to the point, who is prepared to pay the price of doing so?), we would, metaphor after metaphor, tale after tale, ritual after ritual, psalm after psalm, get right away from the opposition of the high and the low, heaven and earth, transcendence and immanence, in order to register in new formulae the sole difference between time to come and passing time, time that fulfils and time that accumulates or ruins. But who will teach us to avert our gaze from the distant, in order to retrieve the near? Who will come and point to the spiritual within the plane of immanence? Who will help us to finally stop talking religion with our eyes turned towards Heaven? There's nothing up there. He is not here. Behold the place where they laid him [Mark 16:6].

It will be said that this speech regime is much too subjective for those in the fold, and much too objective for those who long ago left the fold. It doesn't look as though such a fragile and provisional way of speaking is

168

enough to generate, over space and time, the prodigious elaborations of religion. So how, then, can we say that it's no more a matter of subjectivity than of objectivity, or rather that this particular regime of utterance, like all the others, leaves in its wake its particular form of objects and subjects? No, of course it's not just a matter of some personal, psychological sentiment, heard by the voice of conscience in the intimacy of one's heart of hearts, and making no claim whatever on the form of the external world. Those in the fold would be right to lament such a reduction: religion within the limits of one's innermost conscience. It's because they confused religion and politics that our ancestors had to resort to that extreme solution to stop them tearing each other to pieces in the name of their faith, thereby putting an end to the Wars of Religion. But if the word doesn't reside in the heart, it can't be reduced either to that form of objectivity that finds in scholarly and erudite proofs the path of indisputable reference. Let's let the sciences produce their own objects, remote and reliable, controlled and distant, visible and mediated. They alone know how to convey reference in information. Religious speech, for its part, can only point, through proofs that are indisputable in their way (constantly debated in fear and trepidation), to a perfectly objective phenomenon that will always elude it and that does indeed actually produce new forms of subjection. But the opposition between a (felt, psychological) subjectivity and a (proven, referred) objectivity no longer registers anything of this bringing close together. Who has the energy to revive all the sermons, all the preachings, all the exegeses, all the rituals, so that they stop clumsily tossing the poor advice of psychologists at the clumsy heap of objective proofs, so that they once more become *sacramental*, that is, they quite simply start saying again what they do? Who feels up to fabricating rituals again?

This scrupulous way of gathering meaning will, I'm well aware, be found much too realistic for those on the outside and not materialistic enough for those on the inside. How can we fill the universe with some 'word of God' that would just be a 'manner of speaking'? If by 'cosmic venture' we refer to a table drawn up in front of us that we'd contemplate with our eyes and that would narrate universal history from beginning to end, it'd be better to leave such great narratives to drawers of panoramas, or animators of Omnivision cinemas. You can do a lot with such tables but not reboot the teeniest hint of a beginning of religious sentiment. In any case, the great narratives, the great cosmic panoramas written by scientists who, without flinching, unfold history from the Big Bang right up to *Homo sapiens*, lose sight of the slow and precise work of the sciences as swiftly as 'cosmosifying' leads astray the slow work of religion. If, by cosmic venture, we refer to that form of speech that is not located in front of us but that registers that with which we start to speak, then we can see how at times the great narratives can, in their way, spur on its movement. The way the power of a current of air blowing at your back is revealed to you for a few short moments only if you throw coloured ribbons into it at an angle and from behind, similarly all narratives can be useful if we launch them properly and renew them often. But only if we recognize that the *small* narratives will do every bit as well: an Apocalypse that moves heaven and earth by sumptuous special effects doesn't register anything more than *Babette's Feast*, which stirs up only priceless wines and delicacies. What we can never do anymore is capture, immobilize the sense of presence through some unique, orthodox, disciplined, standardized history, for then one thing is certain: the contents will have escaped. Either you look in the box and it's empty, or it's full but you can't see it.

By putting a cosmic dress over religious expression, you don't get any further or any higher, you don't do anything more grandiose or more profound than if you made it wear the humble veil of your love life. You've registered the same effects across different layers of narrative, that's all; it makes a bit more noise but doesn't necessarily convert any better, any more than the great organs could replace the frail trebles of the recorder. By linking religious utterance to the 'big questions' about the 'ultimate meaning of existence', you hide all that might be unfulfilled in the expression *a* cosmos, *a* 'God'. Those are two over-hasty unifications, made without going to the slightest trouble – especially if we chuck in a 'God' who is the 'creator' of 'the' world, for good measure. Nothing proves there is 'a' cosmos' and everything proves, for sure, that there is not yet 'a' 'God'. No prefix could be more blasphemous than the *mono* of monotheism. Look at the never-ending bloodletting on the stony ground of Jerusalem: never has polytheism, so hated by the clerics, produced so many interlinked crimes, human sacrifices, overlapping idols, blood-soaked altars as those few handspans of loose scree dedicated to the invocation of the 'one God'. Never have Aztec pyramids streamed with so much blood; never have the various

171

pantheons accumulated so many scandalous impieties; never has the name of 'God' been said so often in vain. What Jerusalem demonstrates through the absurd is that 'God' is not one. There you have three tasks that no one has the right to simplify in advance: the unity of a single G.; the unity of the cosmos; the unity of a G. and a cosmos. The virtual people has not yet gathered that is capable of recognizing the unification of those particular presences, through the diversity of times and places. This is because universality isn't behind us, to be preserved or destroyed, but ahead of us, like backbreaking labour in a vineyard that there aren't enough labourers to do [Matthew 20:1-16]. Catholicity does not consist in spreading the good word right to the ends of the universe, but in producing from start to finish and in all places, just through talk that is risky every time, the future demands of a universe still to be negotiated. You can no more speed up the risky production of a single G. than you can decide in advance the size of the virtual people who will make up, at the moment of revival, those who feel they've been brought closer together, saved, resurrected and redeemed.

It's really strange in the end: on the one hand, you have the impression that everything has been gambled, everything lost, that it's all over; on the other, that nothing has really even yet begun. On the one hand, you lie there crushed and mute, your tongue paralysed by the enormity of the task, the antiquity of the texts, the dizzying accumulation of the commentary, the magnitude of the crimes; on the other, you feel like speaking by babbling like a child, as though it was the first time that

an established language became speech. Religious utterance seems to have hit its low-water mark; at the same
time, you get the impression that its high-water levels
are still to come, that it has barely emerged from these
other forms with which it has so long been confused.
On the one hand, no era seems less right for listening to
it than ours; on the other, none has had better acoustics
to hear it with: each word resonates as never before. No
world is as conducive as ours to the revival of the word.
All the obstacles have finally been removed: the fetishes
are in their place, the sciences in their networks, politics
in its own form of faithfulness. What 'belief in God' can
no longer gather in – well, the beautiful vessels of atheist
unbelief are ready to receive it.

In short, it should no longer amaze us: how many
years has it been, how many centuries, since those
professionals of the word, the clerics, found themselves
in a contemporary period that they didn't hate with all
their guts? Idols, materialism, the market, modernism,
the masses, sex, democracy – everything has horrified
them. How would they have found the right words?
They wanted to convince a world they hated with all
their soul. They really believed that you couldn't possibly speak of religion except by first deporting peoples
to other places and other times, supposedly more 'spiritual'. Worse still, they believed that they would only
be judged on their capacity to execrate their era: they
confused the transformation of time by bringing people
close with transmigration to a far-away time made
irrelevant aeons ago. They only succeeded in producing costume dramas, historical epics, on the pretext
of rebooting religious sentiment. A glance at what is

Latour's enemies

derisively known as 'contemporary sacred art' is enough for us to understand this category mistake. As for me, this world suits me down to the ground, I don't know a better one, I don't have any other, what's more. There is no other world, just this one here, the only one we have, to be seized again quite differently.

Why did we lose the use of religious speech? Because we believe religion to be tortuous, as if we needed it to accede to dark and distant mysteries all the way along a narrow path sewn with pitfalls. It does indeed sow obstacles that cause us to stumble, but that's because its ordeals have another spring mechanism: it really is hard, in fact, to find the right words, accurate and precise, to make speech salutary, to speak *well* of the present. I haven't invented anything. In natural or social science, the researcher has a duty to add his stone to the vast edifice of knowledge, to discover, to innovate, to produce new information; but in matters of religion, his duty is faithfulness: he doesn't have to invent but to renew; he doesn't have to discover but to recover; he doesn't have to innovate but to revive the never-ending refrain afresh.

Don't judge me too harshly: despite appearances, I haven't added anything or taken anything away from the treasure of faith, not one comma, not one iota.

I was as faithful as can be. Without a mandate, without any authority, I, who am not even a believer (for it's not about belief), have found only this clumsy, hesitant, self-taught way of celebrating at the same time as others, on the sidelines, for myself alone, without any community, without communion, the Jubilee of the Year 2000.